Popular Justice

SUNY series on the Presidency: Contemporary Issues

John Kenneth White, editor

Popular Justice

Presidential Prestige and Executive Success in the Supreme Court

Jeff Yates

State University of New York Press

Published by
State University of New York Press, Albany

For information, address State University of New York Press,
90 State Street, Suite 700, Albany, NY 12207

Production by Judith Block
Marketing by Anne Valentine

Library of Congress Cataloging-in-Publication Data

Yates, Jeff, 1965–
    Popular justice : presidential prestige and executive success in the Supreme
      Court / Jeff Yates.
      p. cm. — (SUNY series on the presidency)
    Includes index.
    ISBN 0-7914-5447-9 (hc : alk. paper) — ISBN 0-7914-5448-7 (pb : alk. paper)
      1. United States. Supreme Court. 2. Judicial process—United States. 3.
    Presidents—United States. 4. Executive power—United States. 5. Political
      questions and judicial power—United States. I. Title. II. SUNY series in
      the presidency

    KF8742 .Y38 2002
    347.73'26—dc21   2001049807

10 9 8 7 6 5 4 3 2 1

*To my family, who has encouraged me
in every venture that I have endeavored, and
to my wife Rebecca, who provides continuing inspiration
in all that I do*

Contents

Figures

Tables

Chapter One

Introduction

The relationship between the president and the United States Supreme Court is indeed an enigmatic one. Perhaps this is attributable to a lack of consensus over the appropriate parameters of power between these two branches of government. President (and later Supreme Court Chief Justice) William Howard Taft embraced a limited presidential power, stating "the president can exercise no power which cannot be fairly and reasonably traced to some specific grant of power or justly implied and included within such grant as proper and necessary" (Biskupic and Witt 1997, 169). In contrast, President Theodore Roosevelt's "stewardship" theory of presidential leadership envisioned an expansive power in which the president should act on the public's behalf, in Roosevelt's words, "whenever and in whatever manner [is] necessary, unless prevented by direct constitutional or legislative provision" (170). Hence, while Taft envisions a model of presidential action constrained by rules and subject to exacting judicial review, Roosevelt's model of the presidency is one of ample executive discretion and deference from other political actors.

The effective bounds of the Supreme Court's powers are similarly indeterminate. While Chief Justice John Marshal successfully positioned the Supreme Court as the final authority on the Constitution in *Marbury v. Madison*, the practical ability of the Court to function as an effective political force is perhaps open to question. Under the Constitution, the Court has little in the way of direct implementation power and is essentially dependent upon its institutional legitimacy for compliance with its commands. An example of the Court's enforcement quandary and its inherent reliance upon public confidence for its tacit authority is illustrated

1

by Justice Lewis Powell's retrospective comments (in 1988) concerning the Court's order that President Richard Nixon turn over damaging tapes in *United States v. Nixon*. Powell confided that, "one has to wonder what would have happened if Nixon had said what President Jackson said on one occasion, 'You have your decree, now enforce it.' Of course, there was no way we could have enforced it. We had 50 'police' officers, but Nixon had the First Infantry Division" (Powell 1995, 173). In the end the unpopular and beleaguered executive complied and the Court managed to avoid a potentially serious threat to its institutional authority.

Interaction between the president and the Court does not always involve the president as a direct party before the Court as in *United States v. Nixon*. The president and the Court also interface informally in their confrontations over the direction of American legal policy. Certainly presidents hold convictions on many of the policy areas that the Court rules on. While presidents cannot force justices to vote their way, there are informal means by which they can cast their influence on Supreme Court policy-making. Similarly, Supreme Court justices hold their own ideas about the direction of the policies implemented by the executive's bureaucratic agencies, and they review them on a regular basis in Supreme Court litigation.

In this book I examine the interaction in the modern era between these two primary political institutions, the presidency and the United States Supreme Court. I assay the fortunes of presidents before the United States Supreme Court and provide insights as to what factors may influence presidential success in Supreme Court litigation. Of particular interest is the question of whether presidents' fortunes before the Court are affected by the level of prestige (public approval) that they experience while in office.

Several important political considerations are addressed. Fundamentally, if we assume that presidents wish to effectively assert their influence, then it is important to discern whether, and under what conditions, presidential power can be successfully exercised and afforded deference by other political actors (i.e., the Supreme Court justices). Further, judicial scholars assert that judicial decision making can be explained largely by attitudinal, external, and political determinants. Under the constitutional separation of powers framework, the justices of the

Supreme Court may act as either facilitators or inhibitors of presidential power. Thus, it is interesting to evaluate what factors help to explain judicial decision making (for or against the president) in cases concerning presidential power in one form or another. Lastly, a prominent debate within the judicial politics literature concerns whether the Supreme Court acts as a majoritarian or counter-majoritarian institution. Here (chapter 2), I assess whether majoritarian opinion (in this instance, public support for the president) influences Supreme Court justice decision making.

I address the considerations outlined above by testing established theories of presidential political power and judicial decision making from the relevant presidency and judicial politics literature, vis-à-vis political interactions between the president and the Supreme Court. I use these primary theories to help explain presidential fortunes in the Supreme Court in three discrete situations in which the president and Court interact. By examining such theories on president-Court relations across several different contexts, I am able to provide a more generalizable account of presidential power before the Court.

First, I address presidential success with the Court in cases involving the formal constitutional and statutory powers of the president. This section (chapter 3) is inspired by the thoughtful work of Ducat and Dudley (1989a, b), who examined presidential fortunes before the federal district courts in cases concerning the formal constitutional and statutory powers of the executive office. They found that judicial loyalty to the appointing president, case type (foreign vs. domestic), and presidential approval ratings affected presidential outcomes in the federal district courts. I build upon this basic framework to assess the votes of the Supreme Court justices in such "presidential power" cases coming before the Court. In this chapter I assess the impact of presidential prestige (public approval), on justices' support for the president, by considering the president's public approval rating at the time of the relevant event (i.e., when the case comes before the Court). Furthermore, considering the fluctuations in approval that ordinarily occur during presidential administrations, I estimate additionally the effects of intra-administration changes (trends) in presidential approval that occur before the case is decided.

Second, I examine presidential power in the Supreme Court via the federal administrative agencies (chapter 4). Presidential scholars, such as Terry Moe (1991, 1998) and others, have advanced the notion that the federal bureaucracy has become increasingly politicized and has become one of the executive's most valuable tools for implementing his policy preferences. However, as Shapiro (1968) notes, such discourse on the politicization of the federal bureaucracy must take into account the fact that political consternation over partisan-based policy changes in the federal agencies are often resolved in court. While the fortunes of the federal agencies in the Supreme Court have long been a topic of interest for judicial scholars (e.g., Pritchett 1948, Tanenhaus 1960, Canon and Giles 1972, Handberg 1979), few have linked their success levels to presidential politics and none have considered the influence of presidential approval on agency success with the Court. I examine the deference paid to presidents' administrative agencies by Supreme Court justices by assessing the influence of attitudinal, political, and external factors including the impact of presidential prestige.

Third, I look at the ability of presidents to get their substantive policy preferences supported by the Supreme Court justices (chapter 5). By "substantive policy preferences," I mean those substantive policies (e.g., law and order, civil rights, etc.) that the Court's decisions affect, and on which presidents have expressed, in one form or another, opinions or predilections as to preferred case outcomes and judicial policy direction. In order to ascertain whether such expressed preferences are heeded by the justices, it is necessary to develop a method of measuring at least some of the legal policy preferences that presidents seek to effectuate through the Supreme Court. While judicial scholars have traditionally discerned presidential legal policy preferences through anecdotal evidence and party presidential election platforms (see Stidham and Carp 1987), I use an alternative method—presidential policy signaling—to ascertain presidential policy inclinations and priorities. In this chapter I argue that attitudinal, political, and external factors, including presidential public standing, can affect the likelihood that the Supreme Court justices will afford deference to presidents' policy preferences.

There have been numerous assessments of presidential power with regard to the Supreme Court (e.g., Pritchett 1948, Rossiter

1951, Schubert 1957, Scigliano 1971, Corwin 1984, Abraham 1992, Biskupic and Witt 1997). However, with rare exception (Yates 1999, Yates and Whitford 1998, Genovese 1980), such studies have provided essentially qualitative evaluations of executive interactions with the Supreme Court and the individual justices or analysis of specific Court holdings concerning presidential assertions of power. Thus, there is a relative lack of systematic quantitative analysis concerning how the Supreme Court has decided on presidential power. I endeavor to assess presidential power with the Supreme Court by empirically testing hypotheses regarding interactions between the presidency and the Supreme Court justices. Furthermore, my examination of the impact of presidential approval on Supreme Court justice decision making undertakes to provide some insight into the enduring debate on the influence of public opinion on Supreme Court decision making.

Chapter Two

Presidential Prestige and Judicial Decision Making

Presidential influence on the decision making of United States Supreme Court justices has been a timeworn subject of study. Most of the literature on the presidency and the Court has focused on presidents' ability to affect Court policy through the nomination process (e.g., Goldman 1989, Abraham 1992). While some have noted that presidents have been "surprised" by the decisions of their Supreme Court appointments, the majority of studies have found that, on average, presidents have been successful in shaping Court policy through their appointments (Biskupic and Witt 1997, Thomas and Pika 1996, Tribe 1985). Under this theory of president-Court interaction, the president's ability to affect Court policy is manifested fundamentally in his opportunity to appoint like-minded justices to the bench, assuming that his appointments successfully pass the confirmation process.

In short, the president's influence on Court policy-making is only as pervasive as his appointment opportunities. It follows that a president such as Richard Nixon, who had several appointments to the Court, would have more influence on the Court than would Jimmy Carter, who had no nominations. While this theory of presidential power vis-à-vis the Supreme Court provides a partial answer as to how the president can affect Supreme Court policy, it fails to tell us much about how presidents might *contemporaneously* affect Supreme Court justice decision making. In other words, beyond the appointment process, what factors influence the degree to which the justices of the Supreme Court support the president and his policies?

The "attitudinal model" of judicial decision making posits that justices vote their sincere policy preferences in cases, referencing no external sources or influences (see Segal and Spaeth 1993). Hence, the attitudinal model suggests that the only way a president can influence Court decision making is through the appointment process. Some scholars have questioned the conclusiveness of the attitudinal model and argue that external factors are referenced by justices in deciding cases (e.g., Fleming and Wood 1997, Mishler and Sheehan 1993, 1996). In this book I explore the possibility that external factors may affect Supreme Court justices' decision making with regard to the president and his policies. Specifically, I seek to provide insight as to whether justices are influenced by a president's preferences and public prestige in their voting decisions.

Why should justices care about presidents' preferences or public standing? Why should it affect their voting choices in cases? In answering these questions it is effective to examine: 1) the democratic nature of Supreme Court decision making, and 2) how presidential prestige has affected the decision-making of other relevant political actors. First, I will set forth the argument that the justices of the Court are moved by the tides of public opinion generally, and second, I will demonstrate how presidential prestige has been found to influence the decision-making processes of other political actors. Last, I argue that presidential prestige is an important external factor that should be considered when evaluating interactions between the Court and the president.

Public Opinion and the Supreme Court

The democratic nature of Supreme Court decision making has been an enduring, and heated, controversy in judicial politics study. However, in recent years all but a few dissenting voices have come to agree that the Court's opinions generally track public preferences. General consensus has also been reached on the proposition that such congruence between public preferences and Court decisions is, at least in part, due to the impact of presidential appointments (see Mishler and Sheehan 1996, Fleming and Wood 1997). Thus, the debate has turned from questioning whether the Court is majoritarian (Dahl 1957) or counter-majoritarian (Casper 1976) in nature to whether con-gruence between public preferences and Court decisions is due to the direct influence of public opinion, or is merely a function of changes in Court ideological composition through the elected branches of government.

Advocates of the "judicial replacement" hypothesis argue that any correlation between public preferences and Court policy-making is due to changes that occur in the elected branches (Dahl 1957, Funston 1975, Norpoth and Segal 1994). Essentially, the Court is unwilling to overrule the contemporary law-making coalition because the appointment-confirmation process has an inherently electoral connection, and hence the Court's ideologi-cal composition stays in line with majority views (Dahl 1957). Funston (1975) adds that any counter-majoritarian Court behav-ior that occurs can be attributed to realignment after elections and that the Court eventually comes back in line with majority preferences. Norpoth and Segal (1994) explicate the judicial replacement hypothesis in the following manner:

> While justices are not accountable to the populace, presidents and senators, who share the power to choose them, are. What-ever configuration of public opinion elects a president, in par-ticular, could transpire in his or her Court appointments. Given plentiful opportunity to put new members on the Court, a newly elected president can alter the Court's ideological com-plexion. It is not that the justices pay keen attention to public opinion but that they have been chosen by a president (with the advice and consent of the Senate) who presumably shares the public's views (716).

Under this theory, external pressures from the public or other political actors do not sway justices' voting behavior; once on the Court they vote their sincere policy preferences. Thus, the judicial replacement theory is logically aligned with the attitudinal model of judicial behavior. Attitudinal theorists discount the possibility of external influences on justices' behavior. They note that while state judicial officers are elected in some states and thus may be susceptible to external pressures (e.g., Brace and Hall 1990), United States Supreme Court justices are life tenured and typically seek no higher political office and therefore have no reason to be influenced by external factors (Norpoth and Segal 1994).

Advocates of the "political adjustment" hypothesis argue that there is a direct connection between the decision making of the Court justices and public and elite preferences. In other words, the political adjustment theory holds that the Court responds to majoritarian concerns, regardless of its ideological composition. In propounding this theory, Mishler and Sheehan (1993) cite as a classic example, the well-known retreat by the Supreme Court (without membership change) of its anti-New Deal holdings in the wake of popular support for President Franklin Delano Roosevelt's policies and his threat to pack the Court. Similarly, in recounting his experiences as a United States Supreme Court judicial clerk, Chief Justice William Rehnquist (1986) attributes prevailing public mood, and President Harry Truman's low public standing in particular, to Truman's loss before the Court in the famous *Steel Seizure* case. Rehnquist comments:

> Judges, so long as they are relatively normal human beings, can no more escape being influenced by public opinion in the long run than can people working at other jobs. . . . Judges need not and do not "tremble before public opinion" in the same way that elected officials may, but it would be remarkable indeed if they were not influenced by the sort of currents of public opinion which were underfoot in the *Steel Seizure* case (768–69).

While such anecdotal evidence of political adjustment has been plentiful historically, empirical support for the political adjustment theory has only been recently forthcoming.

Mishler and Sheehan's 1993 study found a direct link between public opinion and the liberalism of the Court's decisions, albeit at a five-year lag. However, their work was criticized on theoretical and methodological grounds, particularly for performing aggregate-level analysis (Court outcomes) on individual-level theory (Norpoth and Segal 1994). In later work, Mishler and Sheehan (1996) addressed the issue at the individual level (justice votes) and again found support for the political adjustment hypothesis. Specifically, they found that seven of the fifteen justices examined responded to public opinion at varying lag structures. Link (1995) similarly found a relationship between mass public opinion and Court liberalism in the areas of civil rights and criminal procedure. Additionally, he found that political elites (president and Congress) had an influence on Court liberalism in criminal procedure. Finally, Fleming and Wood (1997) demonstrated that public opinion directly affects the decisions of most of the justices across multiple issues. They note that the effect of public opinion on justice voting can be seen only at the margins, but that justices do respond much faster to public opinion than the findings of Mishler and Sheehan (1996) suggest.

The empirical case for a direct relationship between public opinion and Court decisions is by no means closed, however the evidence provided by the above studies is compelling. It seems that the next logical question is, Why would justices be influenced by public opinion? As stated previously, justices are appointed rather than elected and serve for life tenure during "good behavior" under art. 3, sec. 1 of the U. S. Constitution. Alexander Hamilton proposed in *Federalist Paper* 78 that these two features would insulate the justices from external influences. While no conclusive answer to this question has emerged, sensible explanations for the influence of public opinion on Court policy making have been suggested.

One theory as to why justices follow public opinion is well expressed by the oft-cited quote of Justice Felix Frankfurter in *Baker v. Carr* (1962): "The Court's authority—possessed of neither the purse nor the sword—ultimately rests on sustained public confidence in its moral sanction." Mishler and Sheehan (1993, 1996) assert that justices are concerned with maintaining their collective legitimacy (and authority) and therefore are careful not to deviate in their opinions too far from deeply held public beliefs (see also Caldeira 1991).

Mishler and Sheehan (1993, 1996) further propose that, notwithstanding legitimacy concerns, justices are influenced by public opinion because, quite simply, they are social beings influenced by the actions and events around them. They suggest that, "justices are no less susceptible than other individuals in society to influence by evolving societal norms and values. If, for example, attitudes in the political culture toward the role of women in society undergo significant changes over time, it is unlikely that the attitudes and beliefs of sitting justices can remain permanently immune to these changing mores" (1993, 89).

Chief Justice Rehnquist has noted that Supreme Court justices are human decision makers and, as such, cannot completely ignore the "tides of public opinion" (1987, 98). In similar fashion,

Justice Frankfurter stated that the Court's decisions largely reflect "that impalpable but controlling thing, the general drift of public opinion" (Nelson 1989, 1155).

Of course, the reasons set forth above are not mutually exclusive; either one could be tapping into the underlying social phenomena at issue in some important way. Ostensibly, the groundwork has been laid for the proposition that the justices directly reference external concerns such as public opinion in deciding cases. The rationale for such judicial behavior is derived from plausible social and political explanations, as indicated above. If, in fact, public opinion can affect justices' decision making, then the proposition that presidential prestige may affect presidents' fortunes before the Court appears tenable.

Presidential Prestige and Presidential Power

In *Presidential Power* (1980), Richard Neustadt asserts that Washington political actors are particularly in tune with public opinion because they inherently depend on support from the public, in one way or another (64). This dependance upon public support may be evidenced directly as in the case of votes for members of Congress or, as detailed previously, such dependence could be indirect, as in the case of public confidence in and tacit authority for the Supreme Court. Neustadt asserts that, "dependent men must take account of popular reaction to *their* actions. What their publics may think of them becomes a factor, therefore, in deciding how to deal with the desires of a president. His prestige enters into that decision; their publics are part of his. Their view from inside Washington of how outsiders view him thus affects his influence with them (emphasis in the original; 1980, 64)."

While there is little doubt that differences exist between the justices of the Supreme Court and their elected counterparts on Capitol Hill, similarities also exist that may facilitate development of a general understanding of how political actors are influenced by presidential public prestige. Members of Congress and federal judges have several things in common. Most notably, they are all government servants in that their duty is to serve the public and to deliver good governance. Further, their decisions and actions are subject to public scrutiny and the public holds attitudes towards them (Adamany and Grossman 1983, Caldeira 1986, Caldeira and Gibson 1992). Last, members of the Court, like members of Congress, recognize the political ramifications of their actions and are also influenced by the social and political events and conditions that surround them. Thus, in attempting to discern how presidential prestige may influence the decision making of members of the Court, it is instrumental to first examine how presidential prestige has been found to affect members of Congress.

A long-standing debate in American politics exists regarding the impact of presidential prestige on the president's ability to lead Congress. Although most political scientists concede that presidential popularity has at least some impact on presidential influence in Congress, some scholars seriously question its magnitude (see Edwards 1989, Bond and Fleisher 1990). Others believe that prestige exerts a substantial influence on presidential success in Congress (see Rivers and Rose 1985, Brody 1991, Brace and Hinckley 1992). Whether the effect of prestige on executive success in Congress is considerable or only matters at the margins, it still provides important insight into the nature of presidency-Congress interactions. What is perhaps more pertinent to this heuristic examination of Congress-president relations is not so much the magnitude of influence that presidential prestige yields but, rather, why it has an impact on members of Congress.

One potential pathway of influence is that presidential approval taps into a broader dimension of public attitudes generally. In other words, public approval of the president reflects the country's broader opinions on politics, policy, and good governance (Edwards 1989, Edwards and Wayne 1994). Thus, the president, and especially a popular president, acts as a "cue" for public sentiment and members of Congress respond because they believe that being sensitive to public opinion is an important part of their role in government service (Edwards 1980).

Presidential scholars also suggest that representatives may respond to presidential public standing because they perceive potential political repercussions (e.g., Edwards 1980). A senior aide to President Carter has commented:

> When the president is low in public opinion polls, the Members of Congress see little hazard in bucking him. . . . After all, very few Congressmen examine an issue solely on its merits; they are politicians and they think politically. I'm not saying they make only politically expedient choices. But they read the polls and from that they feel secure in turning their backs on the President with political impunity (Edwards and Wayne 1994, 309).

Similarly, Brace and Hinckley (1992) note that members of Congress and the president are well aware of each other's relative power and public support. They suggest that congressional perceptions of presidential prestige may make members more timid or courageous in dealing with the president. However, they caution that Congress is by no means a "blank slate" on which a popular president can write. Presidents may only wield prestige against the powerful constraints of representatives' ties to their constituencies, who ultimately dictate reelectability (77).

Rivers and Rose (1985) suggest that even highly popular presidents possess few practically viable sanctions that may make a member of Congress more cooperative. They note a bad track record historically of presidential attempts to unseat uncooperative representatives and argue that the development of incumbent constituency services has largely negated any presidential election effects. They assert that "the connection, we believe, rests not on any calculation by the Congressmen of how his constituents will judge his support or opposition to the president's program, but on a sense of "common fate" among Congressmen based on their understanding of how the public holds government accountable for policy failures" (187). Rivers and Rose make a strong case that it is not the threat of presidential retribution that makes presidential prestige influential, but rather that representatives perceive that they share a common public with the president with whom they sink or swim. Thus, we see that there are several viable pathways for the influence of presidential prestige in Congress. Whether these explanations are based on what members of Congress think that they ought to do, or on what members think is in their best interest to do does not change the end result: public popularity of presidents fosters deference toward the president by these political actors.

Presidential Prestige and Supreme Court Justices

The foregoing analysis evinces two fundamental precepts that are relevant to president-Supreme Court interactions: 1) credible and convincing empirical evidence exists to support the proposition that Supreme Court justices care about and are directly responsive to public opinion; and 2) a consensus of studies on president-Congress relations indicates that presidential success in Congress is, to some degree, conditioned upon presidential prestige. These points adjure the question: Are Supreme Court justices responsive to presidential prestige in their choice to support the president and his policies? This question is left largely unanswered by the existing presidential and judicial politics literature.

Mishler and Sheehan (1993) examined the impact of both mass and elite opinion on the liberalism of Court decisions. They assessed the impact of presidential influence on Court decisions by using a dummy variable indicating that a Democratic president was in office and by using a partisan-controlled index of presidential approval. They found that when Court ideological composition was controlled for, presidential approval had no effect on Court liberalism. However, the presence of a Democratic president in office had a positive and statistically significant effect on Court liberalism. Similarly, Link (1995) found that the presence of a Democratic president in office had a positive effect on Court liberalism in the area of criminal procedure. He found no such effect in the area of civil rights, however.

Ducat and Dudley's (1989a) study of presidential power in the federal district courts assessed how the president fared in cases dealing with the formal constitutional and statutory powers of the executive office. Their findings demonstrated that presidents fared better when they were involved in litigation concerning foreign and military affairs and in cases in which they had nominated the judge deciding the case. Furthermore, they found that in domestic affairs cases, district court judges were more inclined to support the president's formal powers at issue in litigation when he was experiencing higher levels of public approval. They note, "As Neustadt argued over a quarter of a century ago, presidential leadership on the home front depends upon his persuasive power backed by his public prestige. *In this area, district court judges have not acted much differently from other officeholders with whom the president deals*" (emphasis added, 116).

Certainly there are distinctions that can be drawn between federal district court judges and Supreme Court justices. However, the similarities between the two should also be considered. Both sets of judicial actors are appointed rather than elected, and both serve for life tenure. Thus, electoral politics concerns and job retention threats are not an issue with either set of judicial officials. Yet, despite the absence of electoral concerns, district court judges are still swayed by presidential prestige. While Ducat and Dudley (1989a) do not offer extended speculation as to why district court judges are influenced by presidential prestige, I submit that Supreme Court justices may be swayed by presidential public standing for some of the same reasons that judicial scholars argue that justices are moved by public opinion generally.

In their study on the etiology of public support for the Supreme Court, Caldeira and Gibson (1992) suggest that, "to persist and function effectively, political institutions must continuously try to amass and husband the goodwill of the public. For the Supreme Court, public support bulks especially large; it is an uncommonly vulnerable institution" (635). Hence, the Court is dependent on public support for its legitimacy, autonomy, and tacit authority. Indeed, retaining such public confidence is vital to protecting the Court's ability to make rulings free from intrusion by the other two branches of government. Chief Justice Rehnquist recently addressed how the Court's institutional protection relies on maintaining public confidence. After recounting a number of historical instances in which the Court's authority and independence had been challenged, but ultimately survived, he concluded: "I suspect the Court will continue to encounter challenges to its independence and authority by other branches of government because of the design of our Constitutional system. The degree to which that independence will be preserved will depend again in some measure on the public's respect for the judiciary" (Rehnquist 2000).

Of course, fostering public good will and support involves paying some attention to what the public wants (Stimson, MacKuen, and Erikson 1995). Congressional scholars suggest that the president's popularity may serve as a surrogate for public opinion generally, and hence members of Congress reference presidential prestige as a means of responding to public attitudes concerning good governance (Edwards 1989, Edwards and Wayne 1994). Given the evidence that the justices of the Supreme Court respond directly to public opinion, it is tenable that justices may similarly tap into such a convenient proxy for popular opinion and public attitudes concerning good governance, especially in their interactions with the president.

Additional theoretical support for the notion of judicial responsiveness to presidential prestige is provided by "separation of powers" scholars. They suggest that interactions among the three branches of government can be analyzed as a formal game in which each branch bases its decisions on sophisticated forward thinking of how the other branches will respond (Epstein and Knight 1998, Eskridge 1991, Gely and Spiller 1990). In a separation of powers game, the president (through his veto power) can emerge as either an ally or opponent to the Court in the event that Congress has executed a statutory override of a Supreme Court decision. Moreover, the Court is dependent upon the executive branch to provide practical enforcement of its decisions. Stimson, MacKuen, and Erikson (1995) suggest that Supreme Court justices may engage in "rational anticipation" in their decision making. They assert:

> First, justices care deeply about substantive outcomes. They also share policymaking authority with elected politicians. When competing with politicians, justices must consider the possibility that their decisions will be overridden or indifferently enforced. They compare the policy outcome that obtains when they choose their "ideal point" and engage political opposition against the outcome likely when they compromise in an effort to avoid active political opposition. Thus, justices who wish to exert authority over the direction of American life will anticipate actions of the other branches of government. Further, institutionally minded justices will want to avoid public defeat and the accompanying weakening of the Court's implicit authority: they will compromise in order to save the institution (555).

Supreme Court justices may rationally anticipate that the president will expressly disobey an order of the Court, as Lincoln did in the *Merryman* case when he refused to follow the order of Chief Justice Taney (Nelson 1989). Similarly, the president can be indifferent in implementing Supreme Court orders, as was the case with Andrew Jackson in the *Cherokee Indian* cases, on which it is reported that he stated, "the Court has made its decision, now let's see them enforce it" (Witt 1990). Alternatively, the executive can actively support the Court in its decisions, as was demonstrated when Eisenhower dispatched federal troops to enforce the Court's decision in *Brown v. Board of Education* (Nelson 1989). Hence, justices can be considered as rational political actors who recognize the interdependence of the branches of government, and understood their own reliance on public confidence in providing authority for their decrees and in protecting them from institutional incursion. This institutional interdependence, along with the Court's inherent need to retain public support to retain credibility and independence, are elucidated aptly by Justice Lewis Powell in his concurring opinion in *United States v. Richardson*: "Repeated and essentially head-on confrontations between the life-tenured branch and the representative branches of government will not, in the long run, be beneficial to either. The public confidence essential to the former and the vitality critical to the latter may well erode if we do not exercise self-restraint in the utilization of our power to negate the actions of the other branches" (418 US 166 at 188 [1974]).

Given that maintaining public confidence is paramount for the Court's independence, tacit authority, and effectiveness, it is sensible that the justices would be inclined to avoid locking horns with a popular executive. Accordingly, we might reasonably expect that rationally acting justices would be more likely to support the actions and policies of a president who is backed by strong public support.

In fact, there is some evidence to suggest that the justices of the Supreme Court can improve their relative public standing and protect their institutional position by engaging in such strategic behavior. Caldeira (1987) uses multiple interrupted time-series analysis to examine the effect of the actions of the president and the justices on public support for President Franklin Delano Roosevelt's plan to restructure the Supreme Court (i.e., "pack" the Court with New Deal-friendly personnel). In a series of decisions during FDR's first term, the Court struck down a number of the popular president's New Deal acts. Reelected by a landslide vote in 1936, FDR set forth a proposal that would allow him to nominate six additional justices to the Court, ostensibly to provide the judicial support necessary for carrying out his New Deal reform. FDR's proposal had serious ramifications for the institutional integrity of the Court, and this confrontation was closely followed by the media and the public. Caldeira analyzes a series of Gallup polls, taken during the months following his proposal, that measured public support for FDR's plan to dilute the Court. He finds that public support for the plan was bolstered by FDR's early attempts to "go public" with the plan through speeches and radio addresses. However, such public support was seriously curtailed by the Court's choice to reverse its anti-New Deal jurisprudence by upholding the Wagner Act in *NLRB v. Jones and Laughlin Steel Company.* This move diminished the perceived need for Court structural reform (in order to get the New Deal implemented) and FDR's plan to alter the Court eventually faltered (1987, 1147–49). Caldeira asserts that, regardless of any alleged jurisprudential motives, the Court's actions played a crucial part in framing public opinion on this matter and ultimately dooming FDR's plan. He concludes that "the Court wisely chose to give up on the substantive issues and protect its structural integrity" (1150).

In sum, the proposition that Supreme Court justices may be responsive to presidential prestige in their decisions to support or oppose the president and his policies is intuitively plausible. Essentially, justices react to the public's support of other government branches due to their nature as social and political beings who care about their institutional independence, legitimacy, and efficacy. If this is found to be the case, even at the margins, then this provides us with tremendous insight into interactions between these two primary institutions, as well as to Supreme Court decision making in general.

Building Models of President-Justice Relations

The theory set forth above quite simply suggests that, in assessing interactions between the Supreme Court justices and the president, it is important to consider the role that the president's public prestige may play in how other political actors (namely Supreme Court justices) treat the president. This is not to say that presidential prestige dictates presidential outcomes or votes by justices in the Supreme Court. On the contrary, one would indeed be ill-advised to not take into account additional factors that could help explain justices' treatment of the president and his policy preferences. The theory spelled out above is not offered to supplant existing theories of judicial decision making, but rather is provided to afford a supplementary explanation for justices' decision making concerning presidential power.

In the chapters that follow I evaluate president-justice relations in three distinct circumstances, or contexts. In each circumstance, I carefully consider the relevant judicial and presidential literature in building explanatory models of interaction between the president and the Supreme Court justices. Thus, the situation in which the president and the justices are interacting helps structure the specification of the explanatory model. Therefore, some variables that are utilized to help explain justices' treatment of the president appear in all three models, while other variables are situationally specific to the particular president-justice interaction being evaluated.

For instance, in chapter 4, I assess the president's success before the Court via his bureaucratic policy implementers, the federal agencies. In evaluating the success of the president's agencies before the Court, I consider the impact of the proximity of the agency (to the president) that is litigating before the Court, consistent with the relevant literature on agency success before the Court (e.g., Sheehan 1992). Of course, this variable is specific to this particular interaction and is not used in other models. However, as stated above, there are some explanatory factors that are used in all three models in one form or another. These general factors are outlined below and provide us with the basic building blocks for evaluating president-justice interactions.

Presidential Prestige

As detailed previously, it is theoretically plausible that Supreme Court justices may be influenced by presidential prestige in their treatment of the president and/or his policies, due to their nature as social and political beings. A steady measure of presidential prestige has been recorded systematically since the late 1940s, in the form of the now familiar presidential approval poll performed by the Gallup Organization. The survey basically asks respondents whether they approve of the job that the president in office is doing. Hence, the percentage of respondents approving of the president's performance in a given survey constitutes the president's "public approval rating." If, as Neustadt (1980) asserts, presidential political power is affected by the president's popular prestige, then it is reasonable to expect that Supreme Court justices may also be affected by the level of public support that the president enjoys in their decisions to support or resist his political practices and policy preferences.

Justice Ideology

Attitudinal theorists claim that Supreme Court justices rely primarily upon their own sincere ideological inclinations, or attitudes, in their voting decisions (see generally, Segal and Spaeth 1993). Few would argue that judicial attitudes do not matter in assessing the voting of Supreme Court justices, and certainly it is imperative to consider judges' ideological tendencies in any model of judicial decision making. However, the pervasiveness and dominance of attitudes in judicial decision making is typically a matter of debate.

Rohde and Spaeth (1976) assert that the impact of justices' ideologies on their voting behavior may diminish in situations in which the Court's institutional authority or the implementation of its decisions are threatened. However, in later work Spaeth notes that such instances occur rarely and points out that the Court's 5-4 decisions in the flag-burning controversy cases in 1989 and 1990 demonstrate that the justices appear ready, willing, and able to vote their ideological preferences even when faced with unified threats from the president and Congress (Segal and Spaeth 1993, 329–30).

In *The Supreme Court and the Attitudinal Model* (1993), Segal and Spaeth strongly assert the conclusiveness of the attitudinal model of judicial decision making, stating that, "A final criticism to which we may be subject more than other attitudinal modelers is our failure to recognize any operative effects on decisions other than those of the attitudinal model. We believe we have sensitively analyzed the relevant internal and external non-attitudinal factors. Their impact on decisions appears to be minimal" (363).

Thus, if we control for the influence of justices' attitudes, then the attitudinal camp would expect that any non-attitudinal explanatory factors (e.g., external influences) would have only a negligible effect, if any, on justice decision making. Of course, if such non-attitudinal factors were found to have a statistically significant effect on justice voting, then the attitudinalists' model of judicial decision making would have to be revised to accommodate any such influences.

Litigation Status

It is also important to consider under what circumstances the president comes before the Court as a litigant. Is the president (or the litigant that he supports) appealing a lower-court loss to the Supreme Court, or is the president being haled into the Court by a disgruntled litigation adversary? While courts generally tend to favor petitioners (parties appealing a lower-court loss) in situations in which they enjoy wide discretion in choosing cases for review, courts also generally tend to favor respondents (parties responding to appeals) in situations in which their discretion regarding case review selection is constrained (Baum 1994). Thus, the litigation status (petitioner or respondent) of the president or the party he favors can be helpful or harmful to him depending upon the level of case-selection discretion that the Court experiences in the particular litigation situation at hand.[1]

The "Two Presidencies" Thesis

The executive's role and power in military and foreign affairs have traditionally been considered more expansive than his role and authority in the domestic policy arena. After all, under the Constitution the president is the commander in chief of the nation's military forces and he has the power to make treaties with other nations (with Senate ratification) and to receive and appoint ambassadors. However, the president's powers in the foreign sphere are not only those formally granted by the Constitution but are also the informal powers that he possesses as the nation's figurehead in foreign relations. In *United States v. Curtis-Wright Export Corporation*, the Supreme Court upheld extensive executive powers in foreign affairs. Justice Sutherland expressly noted in his opinion that "the President alone has the power to speak as the representative of the nation" (299 US 304, 319 [1936]).

Presidential scholars have long debated the notion that presidents have more influence on other political actors when dealing with foreign and military affairs than when dealing with domestic policy concerns. Wildavsky (1966) posits that there are "two presidencies"; a powerful foreign and military affairs leader who receives extensive deference from other politicians, and a less potent domestic leader who must persuade others to support his policy preferences. Most of the two presidencies debate has centered on presidential influence in Congress. However, Ducat and Dudley (1989) found that the two presidencies thesis was confirmed with regard to federal district court judges' treatment of the president in presidential power cases. Given the above, I propose that the policy sphere in which a president is operating (foreign versus domestic) may affect Supreme Court justices' decisions to afford the president deference.[2]

These basic theories of president-justice interaction are combined with more circumstance-specific theories, in the chapters that follow, to help explain justice decision making in three discrete instances of presidential power litigation before the Court. By assessing presidential political power in several contexts, or instances, we can discern how the impact of presidential prestige (and other relevant factors) differ according to the president-Court interaction examined. Through this analysis we can enhance our understanding of executive-justice relations generally and we can learn something about how presidents might more effectively deal with the Supreme Court.

Chapter Three

Supreme Court Support for the Formal Constitutional and Statutory Powers of the President

Does Public Approval Promote Presidential Power with the Court?

My analysis of presidential political power with the Supreme Court begins by examining those situations in which the Court deals directly with the executive office and the legal parameters under which the president functions. Here, I examine the decision making of individual Supreme Court justices in their choice to vote for or against the protection or expansion of the formal constitutional and statutory powers vested in the executive office, during the years 1949 to 1993. These high profile engagements between the president and the Court provide perhaps the most explicit interaction between these two primary institutions in which presidential political power can be evaluated. Thus, my approach centers on the determinants of individual justices' decisions to vote in support of the formal legal powers of the president. I hypothesize that attitudinal, political, and external factors (including presidential prestige) will affect the likelihood that justices will vote to promote the formal powers of the executive office.

This model draws upon the thoughtful work of Ducat and Dudley (1989a) on judicial-executive relations.[3] They endeavored an empirical assessment of federal district courts' support for the executive in cases involving the formal constitutional and statutory powers of the executive. Generally, they found that not only are presidents moderately successful before the federal district courts in presidential power cases, but that their success levels are affected by a set of theoretically interesting factors.

In assessing presidential power before the federal district courts, they quite appropriately derived their predictions from two bodies of literature: judicial and presidential politics. From the perspective of the judicial literature, they argued (and their research substantiates) that various extralegal factors (including presidential prestige and judicial "loyalty" to the president who appointed them) determine presidential success in the federal district courts. Accordingly, their study provides substantial empirical support for the discretionary model of jurisprudence rather than traditional legalistic models, at least in the context of presidential power cases. From the presidential literature, they borrowed the "two presidencies" thesis. That presidential power varies by its context had been previously advanced by various theorists, including Wildavsky (1966) and Justice Sutherland in the *Curtis-Wright Export* case. Under this theory, the president's power is not static, but instead fluctuates. It is most pervasive in foreign and military affairs (the power to command) and less extensive in domestic matters (the power to persuade). Their finding, that the type of power under judicial review matters, supports this hypothesis.

I draw upon Ducat and Dudley's general theories in assessing the voting behavior of United States Supreme Court justices on executive power cases. This allows me to test competing propositions about the nature of judicial decision making. On the one hand, one might expect that Supreme Court justices are freer to vote in accord with their sincere policy preferences than are district court judges. As Segal and Spaeth point out, Supreme Court justices are likely to rely on ideological factors (1993). On the other hand, Supreme Court decisions gain more exposure and are more likely to draw the attention of an engaged executive. Thus, policy-oriented justices may anticipate the actions of the president and act strategically to avoid raising the wrath of the president (Eskridge 1991).

Application of Ducat and Dudley's model to the Supreme Court allows me to test the proposition that the Court acts in a majoritarian manner in supporting popular presidents. It also tests other theories on president-Court interactions, including the two presidencies thesis. Finally, this model allows me to address the fundamental question of the form of the impact of institutional differences across different levels of the federal judiciary. If similarities exist between the two sets of actors (district court judges and Supreme Court justices), then this suggests consistency across different levels of the federal judiciary, at least regarding executive power cases. If differences emerge, however, this provides one more reason to study further the effect of institutional differences between levels of the federal judiciary.

Research Design and Hypothesis Development

I emulate the case collection and selection procedures of Ducat and Dudley (1989a) and assemble a data set with comparable cases by using two primary sources. First I obtained a list of all cases that involved Article I sec. 7, Article II, or Amendments XII, XX, XXII, or XXV in the *United States Supreme Court Judicial Database* (ICPSR 9422). Second, I searched the *United States Supreme Court Digest–Lawyers' Edition* in the general topics of United States, War, and Constitutional Law for cases that mentioned the president or the executive branch, and screened them by selecting those cases in which presidential power was either highlighted in a headnote—point of law—or was discussed in the text of the case. Each case was then read and retained only if presidential power was afforded substantive discussion and was integral to the case's disposition. This yielded thirty-three United States Supreme Court cases from 1949 to 1993 that produced 289 votes by the justices.

The Dependent Variable

The dependent variable in this study is a justice's vote for or against the president, constructed as a dichotomous variable (1 = for, 0 = against). A vote was scored as for the president if it promoted the president's power or protected it from intrusion.[4] Presidents were less successful with United States Supreme Court justices' votes than Ducat and Dudley found them to be with federal district court decisions (Ducat and Dudley 1989a). Whereas presidents won 61% of the time in federal district court, in the

United States Supreme Court they received 54% favorable votes by the justices.[5]

Table 1 displays how the individual presidents fared before the Court. It also provides the distribution of cases from the federal district courts' data for comparison between the two data sets. In addition to an overall lower presidential success rate, there are also differences in presidents' fortunes before the Court.

Table 1. Distribution of Votes in Presidential Power Cases by President*

President	% Votes for– Total Votes [% Cases for– Total Cases]	President	% Votes for– Total Votes [% Cases for– Total Cases]
Truman	60.0% for–25 total votes [66.7% for–8 total cases]	Carter	38.9% for–18 total votes [58.1% for–31 total cases]
Eisenhower	16.7% for–18 total votes [76.5% for–17 total cases]	Reagan	61.4% for–70 total votes [67.4% for–43 total cases]
Johnson	66.7% for–9 total votes [88.9% for–9 total cases]	Bush	64.2% for–53 total votes
Nixon	31.5% for–52 total votes [48.3% for–60 total cases]	Clinton	100% for–9 total votes
Ford	65.7% for–35 total votes [52.9% for–17 total cases]	Total	54.3% for–289 total votes [61% for–195 total cases]

*Numbers in brackets display Ducat and Dudley's (1989) findings for comparison. This study found no cases under the Kennedy administration. In Ducat and Dudley's study, Kennedy had six cases and won five of them.

Whereas Eisenhower was moderately successful before the federal district courts, he was (on a percentage basis) the most unsuccessful president before the Supreme Court. Ford, in contrast, did not fare as well as most of the presidents with the federal district courts, but he was one of the most successful with the Supreme Court. Last, Ducat and Dudley note a decided increase in the number of presidential power cases occurring in the federal district courts in the post-Johnson era. I find a similar increase in presidential power cases in the Supreme Court in the post-Johnson era.

Independent Variables and Expected Effects

FOREIGN/MILITARY AFFAIRS. I divide the policy area of the cases into foreign/military affairs (coded 1) and all other cases (i.e., domestic non-military cases; coded 0). This hypothesis considers the possibility that judicial actors follow clear rules of deference and that the formal powers of the executive office dictate the conditions under which the Court will support presidential power (Ducat and Dudley 1989a, 115).

This thesis is supported by the arguments of rational-choice scholars, who maintain that the executive is ordinarily positioned as the representative and protector of the country in international affairs, usually having more experience in such affairs than do the Supreme Court justices. Therefore, the president has expertise in this area and can gain prestige when he does well. Alternatively, the Supreme Court has little prestige in this area and risks suffering embarrassment by asserting itself as the final sayer of foreign/military policy. Thus, deference is afforded the executive by the Supreme Court in such cases (McGinnis 1993).

It is anticipated that the categorization of a case as foreign/military affairs policy is positively related to the likelihood that a justice will vote in the president's favor. This variable allows me to test the two presidencies thesis in a political area in which it has not yet been systematically examined, the United States Supreme Court.

PRESIDENTIAL APPROVAL. This variable serves as a measure of presidential prestige. I use this variable to test the hypothesis that a president's approval rating is positively related to the likelihood that a justice will vote in his favor. I make operational presidential approval/prestige by taking the average of all Gallup presidential-approval polls occurring in the three months preceding a Court decision.

This variable taps into the theory set forth in detail in chapter 2, regarding presidential approval and deference by political actors toward the executive. If the president can use public approval as a source of capital to promote his influence in Congress (e.g., Rivers and Rose 1985), then is it possible that public approval may influence his success with the Court as well? Similarly, if the Court is responsive to general public opinion trends (Fleming and Wood 1997), then is it also possible that it may be responsive to a well-known public-opinion cue (i.e., presidential approval ratings) in its dealings with the president?

JUSTICE'S PARTY AFFILIATION. Ducat and Dudley (1989) postulated that under the stewardship theory of the presidency, liberal Democrats believe in a strong executive with an ability to cause positive social change through executive assertions of power. Ducat and Dudley tested this theory by hypothesizing that Democratic federal district court judges are more sympathetic to executive assertions of power, but they found no statistically significant relationship.

However, it is important to note that the stewardship or "savior" theory of the presidency is often associated with New Deal Democrats' favorable attitudes toward President Franklin Delano Roosevelt and his successful social welfare policies and leadership in World War II (e.g., Thomas and Pika 1996). Nelson (1995) explains that in this era liberals viewed the presidency as a mobilizing force for the unorganized masses—against wealthy and influential interest groups—as opposed to Congress, who tended to cater to such interests (5–6). Thomas and Pika contend that over time liberals came to believe that "the vast powers of the presidency, which could be used for purposes such as ameliorating domestic social and economic problems and winning World War II, also could be used to wage a futile, costly conflict in Southeast Asia and launch an all-out attack on political 'enemies,' which led to the abuses of Watergate" (1996, 8). Ostensibly, liberals' views toward the presidency have changed since the days of New Deal reforms and World War II. In *The Imperial Presidency*, Arthur Schlesinger (1973) notes a decided trend toward liberals' dissatisfaction with presidential power in the postwar era. Similarly, in *The Accountability of Power: Toward a Responsible Presidency* (1975), Democratic Senator Walter F. Mondale warns against the unfettered use of power by the president, citing claims of past abuses of power such as Vietnam and Watergate. Thus, I depart from Ducat and Dudley here and offer the alternative hypothesis that a justice's affiliation with the Democratic Party is negatively related to the likelihood that the justice will vote in the president's favor.

JUDICIAL APPOINTMENT. I make operational this variable as to whether a particular justice was appointed by the president who was in office when the case was heard (coded 1 if so, 0 otherwise). I use this variable to test the theory that presidents appoint "like-minded" justices, who loyally support that president's politics and practices. Specifically, the inclusion of this variable allows me to assess the expectation that a justice's appointment by a particular president is positively related to the likelihood that the justice will vote in that president's favor.

SAME PARTY. Beyond the possibility that justices are loyal to their appointing president, is it also possible that they are loyal to the political party in which they belong? In other words, are justices more likely to decide cases favorably for presidents who are of their political party? I include the same party variable (coded 1 if so, 0 otherwise) to test the hypothesis that a justice is more likely to vote in favor of presidential power when the justice voting and the president involved in the case are of the same political party.

EXECUTIVE EXPERIENCE. I construct this variable as an indicator of executive political experience (coded 1 if the justice has prior executive experience, 0 otherwise). This variable is used to examine the proposition that a justice's prior executive experience (e.g., attorney general's office, state governor, cabinet member, etc.) may make the justice prone to sympathizing with the president. I use the executive-experience variable to test the hypothesis that a justice's prior experience is positively related to the likelihood that the justice will vote in the president's favor.

Last, this model incorporates dichotomous variables for each presidential administration, leaving out the most predominant administration (most cases) to prevent statistical degeneracy. In this data set, President Ronald Reagan has the most cases and hence is used as the reference category. If we are to assess the presidency as an institution and learn what factors affect the influence of the presidency generally, then it is necessary to control for interadministration deviations that may occur due to characteristics and phenomena attributable to specific presidents.[6]

A Revised Model

I also offer an alternative model to that suggested by Ducat and Dudley in which I propose two measures that may reflect better the underlying factors in which I am interested. I further include a variable—to assess the effect of the presidents' litigation status—that Ducat and Dudley did not consider. First, I am concerned about the impact of ideological factors on the vote choice. A surrogate for Justice's Party is the ideology measure, developed by Segal and others, derived from newspaper editorial accounts of justices' pre-confirmation ideological inclinations (Segal and Cover 1989, Segal, et al. 1995). In this measurement scheme justices are arranged on an ideological scale, with +1 representing the most liberal and -1 the most conservative. I argue that the Segal ideology measure should work in the same way as the Justice's Party variable. Essentially, liberal justices disfavor presidential power and choose to constrain it. I offer the hypothesis that a justice's liberal ideology should be negatively related to the likelihood that the justice will vote in the president's favor.

Second, I include an alternative measure of presidential prestige that takes into consideration the intra-administration fluctuations that occur in presidents' levels of public approval (see Brace and Hinckley 1992). This variable measures the trend in a president's approval ratings by using the same three-month period before the Court decision date. This variable is used as an alternative to the "average approval" variable used by Ducat and Dudley (1989) and is constructed by measuring the change in approval ratings from the first Gallup poll of the period to the last. The measure is analogous to other measures of "overall" presidential approval, which assess the trend of a president's approval by examining the difference between his approval rating upon taking office and his level of support when an event occurs during his administration (Ostrom and Job 1986, James and O'Neal 1991). Thus, this variable allows me to assess intra-administration changes in levels of support for the president rather than just interadministration differences in levels of public approval. Given the substantial attention that has been paid by presidential scholars to how presidents might raise their approval with the public (e.g. Brace and Hinckley 1992), we might pause to question what advantage a president gains with the Court from a rise in the polls. In other words, if a president is on the upswing of public approval, does this translate into political capital in relations with the Supreme Court justices? The approval-trend variable is used to test the hypothesis that a president's increasing approval ratings are positively related to the likelihood that a justice will vote in his favor.

Last, I offer a variable that was not considered by Ducat and Dudley (1989), which addresses the impact of the president's litigation status before the Court. Specifically, I am interested in whether the president fares better with the justices when he appears as a petitioner or as a respondent in Supreme Court litigation. Generally, the Supreme Court exercises extraordinary discretion in the cases it chooses to review and it typically reviews cases that it wishes to reverse (Provine 1980, Segal and Spaeth 1993). Thus, a party petitioning the case (petitioner) is likely, on average, to emerge as the winner under this general rule of thumb regarding case selection (Provine 1980).

Given the above, we might expect that the president would be more likely to receive favorable votes when appearing as a petitioner before the Court. However, in *Deciding to Decide* (1991), Perry argues that while the Court generally exercises considerable discretion over its docket, there are certain "important" cases where it would be "institutionally irresponsible" for the Court to refuse review (280). He notes as an example a presidential power case, *U.S. v. Nixon*. He explains that in these important cases the Court is perhaps not legally compelled to hear the case, but is politically restrained from declining review. Therefore, the Court's ordinarily unrestricted discretion in case selection is inhibited, and the axiom that the Court takes on cases to reverse them may not hold true in this instance.[7] The presidential power cases considered here are typically "high profile" cases. Where the president appears as a petitioner in these cases, he has already lost in the lower court but has decided that the case is worth pursuing in the Supreme Court for one reason or another.

Consequently, the Court is faced with the unenviable choice of either bucking the petitioning president or overturning its colleagues in the lower federal courts. Alternatively, when the president appears as a respondent, he has, in effect, been hauled before the Supreme Court by a litigant that the lower federal court chose not to support. Here, the Court can both support the president and decide consistently with the lower federal court.[8] Thus, in this context, we might expect presidents to fare better as a respondent before the Court. Presidential litigant status is a dichotomous variable (1 = petitioner, 0 = respondent). It is anticipated that, controlling for the other explanatory variables, justices will be less likely to vote in favor of presidential power when the president is petitioning a lower federal court loss.

Estimation and Results

Since the dependent variable in this study is dichotomous, linear regression is inappropriate. Thus, I utilize logistic regression analysis. This maximum-likelihood estimation technique (like probit) reveals the likelihood that a justice's voting decision is conditioned upon the values of the explanatory variables (Brace and Hall 1993). The results of the basic presidential-power model are presented in table 2.

The overall model results indicate that the basic theoretical model of judicial voting on presidential power works reasonably well at the Supreme Court level. The formal goodness of fit test (chi square) indicates that the model is sufficient for explanation (i.e., we can reject the null hypothesis that all of the coefficients but the intercept are zero). Further, the model has fairly strong predictive capability with a reduction in predictive error of 36%.

I find that, consistent with Ducat and Dudley, the Foreign/ Military Affairs variable and the Judicial Appointment variable are both significant and in the predicted direction. Thus, Wildavsky's two presidencies thesis seems to have support in both the lower federal courts and the Supreme Court. The impact estimate indicates that mere categorization of a case as "Foreign/ Military" greatly increases the likelihood that the president will receive deference from the justices. The Judicial Appointment variable result provides support for the notion that judicial loy-

Table 2. Basic Model's Logistic Regression Results for Justices' Voting on Presidential Power

Variable	M. L. E.	S. E.	Impact[a]
Presidential Approval	−.0055	.0132	—
Foreign/Military Affairs	1.4786**	.4153	30%
Justice's Party	−.7120*	.3722	−17%
Judicial Appointment	.6978*	.4064	16%
Executive Experience	.1541	.2948	—
Same Party	−.2734	.3672	—
Eisenhower	−3.2392	.7755	—
Truman	2.1599	.8973	—
Johnson	2.8756	1.0089	—
Nixon	1.5345	.7592	—
Ford	3.7064	.8658	—
Carter	2.8665	.9403	—
Bush	3.8812	.8612	—
Clinton	8.5622	12.2276	—
Constant	.5299	.8436	—

M. L. E. = maximum likelihood estimate; S. E. = standard error
Model chi square = 63.95, df = 14, P < .001
−2 × LLR = 334.53
% correctly predicted = 70.6%
Null = 54.3
Reduction in error = 36%
N = 289

*Significant at .05

**Significant at .01

[a]The impact value displayed is the impact on the probability of a pro-president vote for a one unit change in the value of dichotomous variables (1 versus 0) and a one standard-deviation change in the value of continuous variables while holding all other variables at their mean/modal values.

alty to one's appointing president persists despite the lack of institutional incentives at the Supreme Court level (i.e., possible promotion to a higher judicial position, as Ducat and Dudley speculated might be the case with regard to district court judges). The impact estimate indicates that appointment has a fairly strong influence on the likelihood that a justice will vote to support a president's actions.

In the context of presidential-power cases, the measure of executive prestige (i.e., level of presidential approval ratings) that Ducat and Dudley found to be a significant determinant of judicial deference at the district court level, does not appear to wield a statistically significant influence on Supreme Court justices' treatment of the president. I submit that this may be, at least in part, attributable to the measurement strategy involved here, which essentially taps more into interadministration differences in presidential prestige (among presidents) than into intra-administration changes (trends in specific presidents' prestige). In the next model, I explore the impact of a modified measure of presidential prestige on justice voting.

The coefficient for the Justice's Party variable indicates that indeed, Democratic justices are less likely to defer to presidential power than are Republican justices. Further, the cross-tabulation analysis presented in figure 1 demonstrates that Democratic justices are more likely to vote against presidential power than are Republican justices, regardless of the party of the president in office. This finding provides some empirical support for the qualitative arguments made by many presidential scholars that there has been a fundamental shift in liberal Democrats' attitudes toward the presidency in the post-war era. Furthermore, as figure 1 indicates, Democratic skepticism of presidential power is not attributable to inter-party conflict between justices and presidents. Figure 1 shows that Democratic justices consistently vote against presidential power more often than Republican justices, regardless of the party of the president in office. The Impact estimate denotes the strong effect of partisan affiliation on justices' decisions to support presidential power. I also find, as did Ducat and Dudley at the district court level, that neither Executive Experience nor Same Party exert a statistically significant effect on justice voting on presidential power.

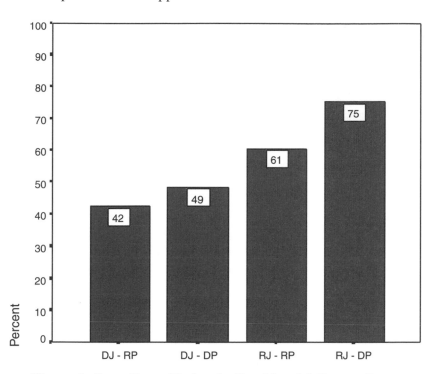

Figure 1. Inter-Party Voting in Presidential Power Cases

Note: DJ = Democratic Justice
        DP = Democratic President
        RJ = Republican Justice
        RP = Republican President

The overall model results for the revised model, displayed in table 3, are quite compelling. The formal goodness-of-fit test (chi square) indicates that the model is sufficient for explanation and the model has excellent predictive power with a 49% reduction in predictive error. Beyond the overall model results, the maximum likelihood estimate coefficients provide several interesting results.

First, the Presidential Approval Trend variable coefficient indicates that the Supreme Court justices are responsive to trends in presidential prestige in their decision to vote for or against presidential power. This finding has significant ramifications for both presidency and Supreme Court study. It demonstrates that

Table 3. Revised Model's Logistic Regression Results for Justices' Voting on Presidential Power

Variable	M. L. E.	S. E.	Impact[a]
Presidential Approval Trend	−.1300**	.0307	21%[b]
Foreign/Military Affairs	1.8235**	.4395	36%
Justice Ideology	−.6716**	.2513	−11%[c]
Judicial Appointment	.5787	.4287	—
Executive Experience	.3653	.3132	—
Same Party	−.1941	.3304	—
President Petitioner	−.9209**	.3233	22%
Eisenhower	−3.8213	.8120	—
Truman	2.9093	.8146	—
Johnson	3.5866	1.0103	—
Nixon	2.1799	.7772	—
Ford	5.5180	.9747	—
Carter	5.6099	1.1572	—
Bush	5.5207	.9939	—
Clinton	9.9838	12.1517	—
Constant	−.1793	.4281	—

M.L.E. = maximum likelihood estimate; S. E. = standard error
Model chi square = 95.16, df = 15, P < .001
−2 × LLR = 303.31
% correctly predicted = 76.47%
Null = 54.3%
Reduction in error = 49%
N = 289

*Significant at .05

**Significant at .01

[a]The Impact value displayed is the impact on the probability of a pro-president vote for a one unit change in the value of dichotomous variables and a one standard-deviation change in the value of continuous variables while holding all other variables at their mean/modal values.

[b]The approval trend measure ranges from −15 to 20 and has a mean of −1.88. A one standard deviation change in the measure is 6.86.

[c]The Segal, et al. (1995) measure for justice ideology ranges from −1 to +1 and has a mean of −.03. A one standard deviation change in the measure is .69.

presidents can improve their fortune with the Supreme Court justices by increasing their public prestige. The impact estimate indicates that the typical swing in presidential approval (one standard deviation—6.86) can bring about a substantial increase (21%) in the likelihood that a justice will vote to support the president. Neustadt's (1990) general assertion that presidential persuasiveness and prestige are tantamount to presidential power is supported by this finding, at least with regard to the Supreme Court justices.

As in the basic model, the coefficient for the Foreign/Military Affairs variable indicates that presidents fare much better in the foreign policy sphere than in the domestic arena. Again, the impact estimate for this variable indicates that the categorization of a case as foreign policy greatly increases the president's chances for success with the Court. Particularly in this policy area in which "the promontories of executive power are carved from solid bedrock" (Ducat and Dudley 1989a, 115). The coefficient for the Justice Ideology variable indicates that liberal justices generally disfavor presidential power (as was found with the Justice Party variable). Thus, consistent with the attitudinal model (Segal and Spaeth 1993), justices do appear to bring attitudinal predilections to the bench when deciding cases concerning presidential power. Again, the Executive Experience and Same Party variables do not approach significance. Also, the Judicial Appointment variable does not quite attain statistical significance at conventional levels of significance in this model (although it is significant at the .10 level).

Finally, the coefficient for the President Petitioner variable demonstrates that the president fares much better with the Supreme Court justices when he appears as a respondent rather than as a petitioner. Given the previously noted political constraints on the Court's discretion to hear presidential power cases, this finding is in line with courts' general tendencies to affirm lower court decisions where their discretionary jurisdiction is restricted or non-existant (Baum 1994). The impact estimate for this variable indicates that the president's litigation status has a considerable effect on the likelihood that a president will be supported by the justices. Presidents who force the Court's hand by petitioning for review appear to suffer for their assertiveness when the justices make their voting decisions. Thus, the president's fate before the Court may be predetermined, to some degree, by the political dynamics that govern whether he appears before the Court as a petitioner or as a respondent.

Possible Selection Effects

Given the statistically significant effect of the president's litigation status (petitioner or respondent) demonstrated above, could it be that indeed the president's fate before the Court is shaped at least in part by the selection process that brought him before the Court in the first place? Figure 2 details the selection process that dictates whether the president appears before the Court as a petitioner or as a respondent. As suggested above, the Court's discretion to hear high-profile cases involving the president may be politically constrained. Hence, the likelihood that the president may appear as a petitioner or as a respondent may be largely attributable to the president's decision to appeal his case to the Supreme Court.[9] Perhaps ironically, presidents appear to be more successful with the Court justices when they are hauled into the Supreme Court by litigation adversaries than when they aggressively petition the Court to hear their case. Thus, presidents may be doing somewhat of a disservice to themselves by "forcing" the Supreme Court to rule on cases that it is politically constrained from declining for review. Consequently, I endeavor to assess whether a strategic selection process may be influencing the president's litigation status (and consequently his success) before the Court.

In order to determine whether such a selection effect may be present, auxiliary-logistic regressions were performed consistent with the procedure suggested by Heckman (1979).[10] Heckman proposed a procedure to determine whether selection effects were present in regression analysis. His procedure entailed analyzing the phenomenon that was theorized to be influencing the process under examination. Here, that phenomenon would be the president's litigation status. He further explained that we can use information obtained from this analysis to determine whether a selection process is present in the primary process that we are examining through regression analysis. Here, of course, the primary process being examined is the likelihood that the justices will vote in favor of the president. The results of these auxiliary regressions are presented in table 4.

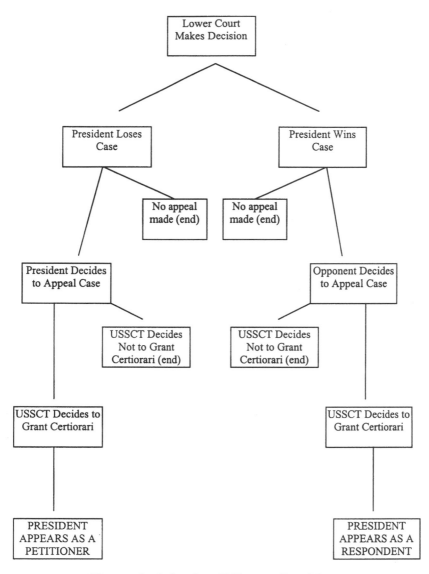

Figure 2. Selection Effects—Presidents

Thus, step one of the procedure involves the development of a model to help explain the likelihood that the president will appear before the Court as a petitioner rather than as a respondent (1 = president appears as petitioner, 0 = president appears as a respondent). In this estimation it is assumed that presidents

Table 4. Presidential Selection Effects—
First and Second Step Logistic Regression Results

Step One Regression—The Likelihood that Presidents Will Appear as Petitioners			Step Two Regression—The Likelihood that a Justice Will Vote for a President		
Step One Variables	M. L. E.	S. E.	Step Two Variables	M. L. E.	S. E.
President Approval (lag 1 yr)	.0574**	.0224	Trend in President Approval	.1598**	.0630
Constit. Law Issue	−2.2867**	.5943	Justice Ideology	−.9215**	.3642
Court Agenda	−9.8279**	1.8041	President Appointment	.3113	.6260
Intercept	−8.9103	21.3343	Executive Experience	.5873	.4644
—	—	—	Same Party	−.0724	.4647
—	—	—	Foreign	1.5872**	.6644
—	—	—	Predicted Probs.	1.0694	1.2960
—	—	—	Intercept	−2.8442*	1.3027

M.L.E. = maximum likelihood estimate
S.E. = standard error

Note: Presidential Dummy Variables are not displayed.

Chi square = 156.75 P < .01
Reduction in error = 52%
N = 289

*Significant at .05

**Significant at .01

M.L.E. = maximum likelihood estimate
S.E. = standard error

Note: Presidential Dummy Variables are not displayed.

Chi square = 50.56 P < .01
Reduction in error = 52%
N = 140

*Significant at .05

**Significant at .01

will petition cases when they feel that they are likely to win, and when the case is important to them. In this auxiliary-logistic regression, it is hypothesized that: 1) presidents experiencing higher levels of approval will be confident as to potential litigation outcomes before the Court and hence, will be more likely to bring a case to the Court (i.e., appear as a petitioner);[11] 2) cases involving constitutional law issues will be more important to the president and consequently he will be more likely to bring such cases to the Court; and 3) presidents will be less likely to appeal cases to the Court when the Court's ideological composition is liberal since, as previously shown, liberal justices tend to disfavor presidential assertions of power.

The results of this auxiliary regression indicate that presidents are more likely to appear as petitioners when they are experiencing high public approval. This finding suggests that presidents act strategically by appealing lower court losses when they possess political capital, namely high public approval. The findings on the constitutional-issue hypothesis were counterintuitive. Presidents were less likely to appear before the Court as petitioners when the case involved a constitutional-issue. Last, as expected, presidents are less likely to appear as petitioners when the Court's ideological composition becomes more liberal. The predicted probability estimates from this regression are saved and used as a regressor in the next model (primary model) to determine whether a selection effect is present in the primary process that we are examining (whether justices will vote in favor of the president).

In step two of the procedure I examine the subpopulation of cases in which the president actually appears as a petitioner. Here, the basic specification used previously to determine what factors affect whether the justices will vote for or against the president is used. Additionally, the predicted probabilities from the step one auxiliary regression are used as a regressor. Here, the predicted-probabilities regressor is used to test the hypothesis that a selection effect is present in the regression analysis at issue (i.e., the revised model on the determinants of justices voting for or against the president). Here, I find that the predicted-probabilities regressor variable does not approach statistical significance and thus, there appears to be no selection effect present in the basic regression analysis. However, it is important to note that the selection model utilized here is rather rudimentary, especially considering the highly complex selection process detailed in figure 2. Therefore, the results outlined here are certainly not dispositive with regard to this issue. Extended exploration of executive branch case-selection strategies have been dealt with in other work (Zorn 2001, 1997a, 1997b) and is beyond the scope of this study.

Discussion

Presidential power and influence have been empirically analyzed with regard to many political contexts—including congressional decision making, voting in congressional elections, and public-opinion direction. This model of justice voting behavior applies established theoretical hypotheses from the presidential and judicial literatures to interactions between the presidency and Supreme Court justices. It empirically tests the proposition that attitudinal, political, and external factors (including presidential prestige) affect the likelihood that Supreme Court justices will choose to support the formal powers of the president. The finding that Supreme Court justices are responsive to presidents' public-approval ratings, in their decisions to vote for or against presidential power, provides support to the general proposition advanced by recent scholars (Mishler and Sheehan 1996; Flemming and Wood 1997) that justices reference public opinion in their voting decisions. Furthermore, the effective application of Ducat and Dudley's theories of trial-judge behavior to the decision making of Supreme Court justices suggests regularity and predictability in federal judicial interactions with the executive.

Moreover, the results from this model provide information with which presidential scholars might speculate as to what is viable presidential strategy in interactions with the Supreme Court. The analysis concerning selection effects tends to suggest that presidents are already engaging in such strategic behavior.

One of the primary strategies that can be employed by presidents in their interactions with the Supreme Court concerns the decision of whether to bring a case to the Court. When losing at the lower federal court level, presidents can either appeal their loss to the Supreme Court or essentially accept the loss as it stands. The results of the litigation status variable indicate that presidents would be advised against forcing the Court's hand by petitioning the Court to overturn the decisions of their lower court brethren. As noted previously, the Court is often politically constrained from declining to review cases in which the executive's powers are directly at issue (see Perry 1991), and therefore is generally inclined to affirm lower court decisions (Baum 1994). Perhaps it is better to settle for a lower court loss than to have the decision affirmed by the Supreme Court and hence, make powerful legal precedent that permanently undermines the powers of the executive office. On the other hand, presidents who are hauled into the Supreme Court by disappointed litigation opponents stand a good chance of having their lower federal court victories supported by the Court. Therefore, unless a president has compelling reasons to believe that an appeal will be well-received by the Court, a reactive litigation strategy with the Court, rather than a proactive one, may be appropriate.

Furthermore, the theories of presidential scholars (e.g., Thomas and Pika 1996) that liberals are skeptical of presidential power are corroborated by the analysis presented here. Thus, presidents (regardless of their partisan affiliation) might think twice before taking their case before a liberal Court. Figure 1 suggests that a Republican-dominated Court is more likely to support a Democratic president's actions than a Democratic-dominated Court. Thus, the partisan/ideological makeup of the Court may provide the president a clue as to his likelihood of success in a presidential power case. Additionally, presidents should also consider the type of presidential power that is at issue in the case. The results of this chapter indicate that there are indeed two presidencies with regard to justices' treatment of the president in presidential power cases. Presidents appear to fare much better with the justices in the foreign policy sphere, where traditional mores of democratic governance favor deference toward the executive.

Beyond case selection, what else can presidents do to improve their lot before the Court? Some support for the notion that justices loyally favor their appointing president is found here.[12] However, presidents often have limited opportunity to appoint Supreme Court justices (e.g., Jimmy Carter) and therefore the occasion for such strategic action is restricted. The findings in the revised model suggest that while general levels of public support for a president do not equate to political capital in justice relations, trends in public support do make a difference. As has been found with regard to Congress-presidency relations, public support (here, trend in support) for the president fosters deference by political actors toward the executive. Consequently, presidents may improve their likelihood of success in presidential power cases by having the increasing support of the people behind them.

In sum, interactions between the Court and the president concerning the president's formal powers are influenced by a variety of factors, including presidential prestige and the justices' ideological inclinations. The model set forth in this chapter provides us with generalizable theories concerning these high-profile engagements between the executive and the Supreme Court. This is significant in that it helps us to understand the presidency as an institution rather than a string of individual personalities having specific relations with the Court.

Chapter Four

Presidential Power Via the Federal Agencies

Presidential Approval and Justice Voting on the President's Bureaucratic Policy Implementers

The analyses presented in chapter 3 indicate that political, attitudinal, and external factors, including presidential prestige, influence the fortunes of the president in Supreme Court litigation where his formal powers of office are at issue. However, the president does not work in solitude. He often advances his political and policy preferences through his bureaucratic agents, namely the federal administrative agencies. Hence, in assessing the presidency as an institution, it is necessary to consider these important policy actors.

The federal bureaucracy provides perhaps the most viable avenue for promoting administration policy direction that is available to the executive (Rourke 1991, Moe 1991). Since legislation generally provides a great deal of discretion in its implementation, presidents can often assert their policy preferences through strategic political appointments in the executive agencies and to a lesser extent in the independent agencies (Rourke 1991, Devins 1994).

Moe (1991) and others maintain that the federal administrative agencies have become politicized and have emerged as a primary means of partisan-based presidential policy implementation. Moreover, presidential scholars believe that this politicization, or "presidentialization" of the federal bureaucracy has increased over time (Rourke 1991; Moe 1998). It could be that this politicization of the federal bureaucracy is a result of presidents seeking political control to achieve the policy goals for which the electorate holds them ultimately accountable. While such public expectations may in some instances be unreasonable, the public's perception of a president's ability to govern, and ultimately a president's historical legacy, may be dependent on his ability to meet these expectations. Moe argues that presidents are ultimately interested in effective political leadership and in order to be an effective leader and achieve policy goals they need a responsive institutional structure that will implement their policy preferences—in short, a politicized bureaucracy (Moe 1991, Moe and Wilson 1994).

The President, Federal Agencies, and the Supreme Court

The federal courts play an important monitoring function over the federal agencies in that they regularly review agency actions. Shapiro (1968) argues that the decisions of the Supreme Court in reviewing bureaucratic action are often political themselves, in that issues concerning the lawfulness of agency action are typically inextricably tangled with value-laden perceptions of how agencies "ought" to be making policy. In short, political strife over bureaucratic policy-making is often resolved through litigation and therefore, to properly assess the "presidentialized" bureaucracy, we must consider the influence of the Supreme Court.

The fact that Supreme Court justices are cognizant of presidents' use of the federal agencies to advance their political preferences is evident in the opinion of Justice Rehnquist in *Motor Vehicle Manufacturing Association v. State Farm Mutual Insurance:*

> The Agency's changed view of the standard seems to be related to the election of a new President of a different political party. . . . A change in administration brought about by the people casting their votes is a perfectly reasonable basis for an executive agency's reappraisal of the costs and benefits of its programs and regulations. As long as the agency remains within the bounds established by Congress, it is entitled to assess ad-

ministrative records and evaluate priorities in light of the phi-
losophy of the administration.(463 US 59 [1983]).[13]

This passage suggests that members of the Court acknowledge
the "presidentialization" of federal bureaucratic policy-making,
and that a number of them endorse it. This sentiment is echoed
in Justice Stevens's opinion for the Court in *Chevron U.S.A. v.
Natural Resources Defense Council, Inc., et al.*, in which he notes that
in making bureaucratic decisions an agency may "properly rely
upon the incumbent administration's views of wise policy to in-
form its judgments" (467 US 865 [1984]).

While the fortunes of the federal agencies in the Supreme
Court has been an enduring topic of interest for judicial scholars
(e.g., Canon and Giles 1972), few have examined the linkage
between agency-Supreme Court litigation success and the presidency. In this chapter I examine presidential power via the federal agencies before the United States Supreme Court, and assess
whether the Court serves as a constraint on executive efforts to
"presidentialize" federal bureaucratic policy-making. My primary
research premise is that the ability of the president's agencies to
be successful before the Supreme Court is conditioned upon the
public prestige of the president in office.

Early research on federal agencies before the Court focused
on agency typology as a determinant of agency success. These
scholars hypothesized that while agencies were generally highly
successful before the Court, certain types of agencies (i.e., economic agencies) were more successful than others (social agencies). However, the economic versus social agency distinction has
proven to be a weak explanation for agency success before the
Court (Crowley 1987, Sheehan 1990, 1992).

More recent work on agencies before the Court has emphasized the role of the ideological direction of agency decision
making. Consistent with the attitudinal model of judicial decision making, it has been found that justices are more apt to rule
against agencies when agency action does not comport with their
sincere ideological preferences (Sheehan 1990, 1992). Sheehan's
(1992) work makes perhaps the first viable connection between
presidential politics and agency litigation success before the Court.
He asserts that the independent regulatory agencies (less proximate to the president) are more likely to receive deferential review

by the Supreme Court than are executive agencies (which are more proximate). Such differences in treatment are based upon the insulation of the independent regulatory agencies from White House politics. Also, their quasi-judicial nature typically affords them favorable standards of judicial review (e.g., the substantial evidence doctrine). Executive agencies, on the other hand, are administrative in nature and are more closely tied to the partisan political concerns of the president in office. Indeed, Sheehan's (1992) findings indicate that the proximity of an agency to the president is significant even when controlling for the ideological directionality of the agency's decision making and Court composition over time.

This study examines competing explanations for justices' treatment of the federal agencies in Supreme Court litigation. It also expands upon the aforementioned link between the presidency and agency success before the Court by considering the influence of presidential prestige on agency success with the Court. In other words, does presidential capital, in the form of public approval, make Supreme Court justices more deferential toward the president's bureaucratic agents in Supreme Court litigation?

Research Design and Hypotheses Development

This analysis of the fortune of the president's agencies before the Supreme Court covers the years 1953 to 1995. It utilizes the *U.S. Supreme Court Judicial Database,* developed by Harold Spaeth (ICPSR 9422). The population of justices' votes considered in this study consists of votes from Supreme Court cases involving three mutually exclusive categories of agencies: independent regulatory agencies, cabinet agencies, and non-cabinet foreign/military policy agencies.

Prior studies (e.g., Crowley 1987, Canon and Giles 1972) have evaluated selected types of agencies, such as independent regulatory agencies, to the exclusion of other agencies. Sheehan (1990, 1992) conducted perhaps the most comprehensive studies on agencies before the Court, including cases that involved all agencies that appeared before the Court. Here, I consider three categories of agencies and exclude other agencies that do not belong to these categories (independent regulatory agencies, cabinet agencies, and non-cabinet foreign/military affairs agencies). While this research design decision does involve some restriction in the scope of my analysis, I feel that such restriction is outweighed by the precision in analysis that is gained in the straightforward comparison among these three types of agencies, rather than considering them against an amalgamated "other" category.[14]

The population of justices' votes is further restricted to votes that can be defined on an ideological dimension as being either liberal or conservative. Thus, cases that turned on issues (as delineated under the Spaeth Supreme Court Data Set Codebook) that were conducive to coding along ideological dimensions were retained. These issues include: criminal procedure, civil rights, First Amendment, due process, privacy, unions, and economic activity. Cases that were not retained turned on issues that were not conducive to ideological coding. These issues include: attorneys, judicial power, federalism, interstate relations, federal taxation, and miscellaneous others. These issues were not conducive to ideological coding because their outcomes often turned on procedural rather than substantive factors.[15]

Agency Litigation Participation and Success

Agency litigation participation before the Court has remained fairly steady over time, constituting between 12% and 20% of the cases on the Court's docket.[16] Figure 3 shows a decline in agency participation after the Eisenhower administration, followed by a rise during the Johnson administration. The participation rate is then stable until the Reagan era, at which point there is dip in participation that continues through the early years of the Clinton administration. Figures 4 and 5 depict the distinctive participation rates of the independent regulatory agencies, cabinet agencies, and foreign policy agencies. The figures indicate a decided decline in the participation rate of independent regulatory agencies over time. The cabinet agencies appear to increase markedly in participation after the Johnson administration, with a slight downturn with Reagan's term and thereafter.

It is tempting to speculate that the decline in agency litigation participation before the Supreme Court (especially with regard to the independent regulatory agencies) is due to the deregulation policies of the Reagan and post-Reagan administrations.

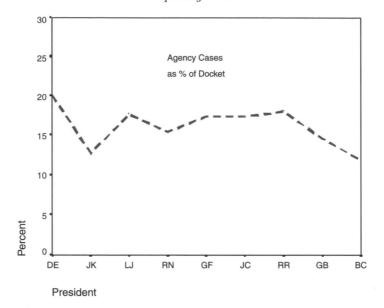

**Figure 3. Agencies Appearing Before the Court
as a Percentage of the Entire Docket**

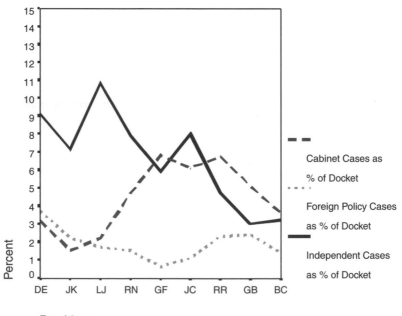

**Figure 4. Type of Agency Cases Before the Court
as a Percentage of the Court's Total Docket**

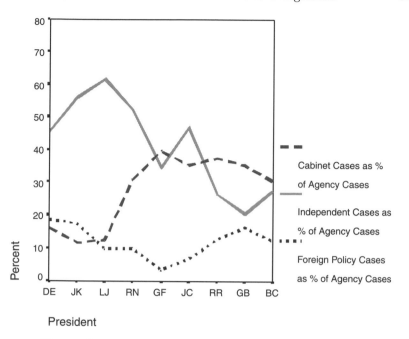

**Figure 5. Type of Agency Cases Before the Court
as a Percentage of All Agency Cases**

However, such an assertion cannot be made with confidence. The fact that the federal agencies appear less often before the Court than in previous years could be due to a multitude of factors including: agencies' propensity to appeal lower court losses, agency opponents' propensity to appeal lower court losses, and the Court's inclination to grant certiorari to agency-related appeals.[17] Similarly, given the assertions of Moe (1998) and others that there has been an increasing politicization of the president's agencies, it could be inferred that the increasing participation of the cabinet agencies before the Court over time is the result of legal consternation over presidential policy changes in these agencies that are the closest to White House concerns. However, while this trend is suggestive of Moe's politicized bureaucracy, such increases in participation before the Court could be ascribed to a multitude of factors, including Court certiorari discretion.

Figure 6 provides a representation of how well the federal agencies have fared before the Court during the time period studied. Figure 6 shows that while the success of the federal agencies has

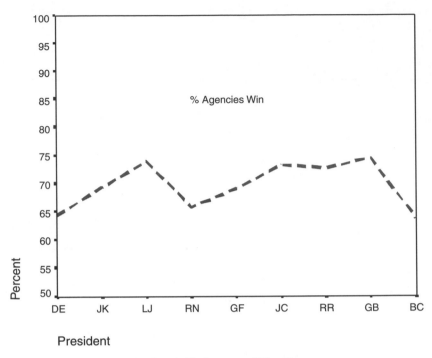

Figure 6. Overall Agency Win Percentage

varied over time, they have basically been substantially successful in Supreme Court litigation. Figure 7 provides a more detailed view, showing the relative success rates of cabinet
agencies, independent agencies, and foreign policy agencies.
Independent agencies appear to have been consistently successful over time, while cabinet agencies and foreign policy
agencies have generally experienced a rise in their success
rates over time. If, as Moe (1998) asserts, the bureaucracy has
increasingly become the vehicle of partisan presidential concerns, then the Court does not appear to have emerged as a
check, but rather as a facilitator of presidential bureaucratic
influence.

Model Specification

While case outcomes provide a valuable visual tool for assessing agency success before the Court over time, the unit of

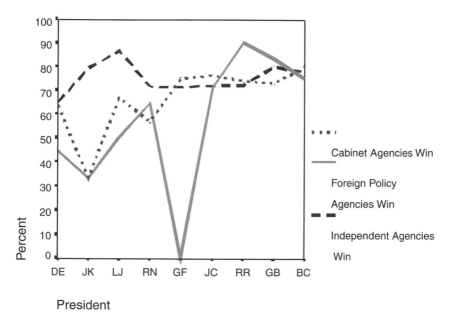

President

* Note: There were only two foreign policy cases
during the Ford administration and both were losses

**Figure 7. Agency Win Percentage:
Cabinet, Independent, and Foreign Policy Agencies**

analysis for this study is justice voting. Using this unit of analysis
allows exploration of the individual-level factors that influence
justice decision making as well as factors general to all of the
justices. The dependent variable in this model is dichotomous,
with 1 denoting that a Supreme Court justice voted in favor of
an agency and 0 denoting that a justice voted against an agency.
I again employ logistic regression analysis, which is an appropriate method for analyzing dichotomous dependent variables
(Aldrich and Nelson 1984).

    In assessing Supreme Court justices' voting in agency cases,
I draw upon the theoretical specification suggested by Ducat and
Dudley (1989a) in their examination of the voting behavior of
federal district court judges in presidential power cases. To tailor
the model to the specific Court-executive interaction at hand, I
also draw upon the previously discussed literature concerning
agency success before the Court.

PRESIDENTIAL APPROVAL. The primary variable of theoretical interest to be tested is presidential prestige, measured here as Presidential Approval. I hypothesize that the Supreme Court's treatment of the president's policy implementers, the bureaucratic agencies, will improve when the president enjoys higher levels of public approval. I make operational this variable as the annual average of the Gallup presidential approval polls for each of the forty-three years in which these Court decisions occur (see figure 8).[18]

FOREIGN/MILITARY AFFAIRS. To test the two presidencies thesis with regard to presidential bureaucratic success before the Court, I consider an agency typology that has not previously been explored in the judicial literature on federal agencies. Under Wildavksky's (1966) thesis, it is expected that agencies that deal with foreign and military affairs policy issues will fare better before

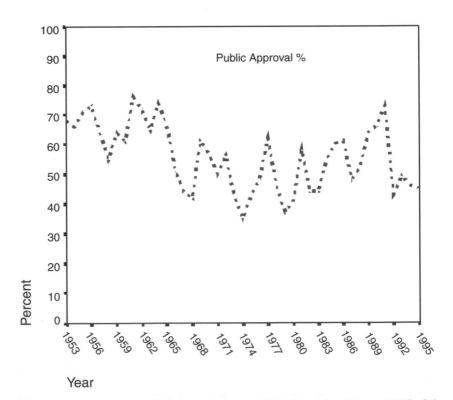

Figure 8. Presidents' Public Approval Ratings by Year, 1953–95

the Court than those agencies dealing with domestic policy issues. This is a dichotomous variable (1 = Non-Cabinet Foreign/ Military Affairs Agency, 0 = Cabinet Agency or Independent Regulatory Agency).[19]

JUDICIAL APPOINTMENT. This variable indicates whether a particular justice was appointed by the president who is in office when the case is heard (1 = appointed, 0 = not appointed). I use this variable to test the theory that justices are loyal to the presidents who nominated them and that they consequently support that president's politics and practices through his bureaucratic agents.

SAME PARTY. It is intuitively plausible that justices who are of the same party as the president in office are more likely to support his bureaucratic politics. This variable is employed to assess the proposition that a justice who shares a president's political affiliation will be more likely to vote in the president's agencies' favor (1 = same party, 0 = different party).

EXECUTIVE EXPERIENCE. It is also quite plausible that a justice's prior executive branch experience (e.g., Attorney General's office, state governor, Cabinet member, etc.) may make the justice prone to sympathizing with the president and executive bureaucratic policy-making. I use the executive branch experience variable to test the hypothesis that a justice's prior experience (1 = executive experience, 0 = no executive experience) is positively related to the likelihood that the justice will vote in the bureaucratic agency's favor.

AGENCY-JUSTICE IDEOLOGY. This variable is used to examine whether the ideology of the justices affects their decisions to vote for or against the agencies in Supreme Court litigation. It is anticipated that a justice's treatment of an agency bringing a liberal case to Court will differ according to the justice's sincere ideological inclinations. This variable is assessed as an interaction term in which the ideological directionality of the agency's previous administrative decision (i.e., the case that the agency brings to the Supreme Court) is considered in tandem with the justices' ideological predilections. Thus, the interaction term is: agency direction[20] (1 = liberal agency decision, and 0 = conservative agency decision) multiplied by the justice's ideology. Justices' ideological inclinations are measured as (per Segal, et al. [1995]) ideology scores and range from 1 (most liberal) to −1 (most conservative). Thus, when an agency brings a liberal case to the Court it is expected that a more liberal justice is more likely to vote to support that agency than a conservative justice. Accordingly, when an agency brings a conservative case to the Supreme Court, it is expected that a more liberal justice would be less likely to vote in support of the agency than would a conservative justice.

AGENCY PROXIMITY. Prior research suggests that the proximity of the agency to the president affects the success of the agency before the Court (Sheehan 1992). Thus, the independent regulatory agencies should fare better before the Court than the president's cabinet agencies.[21] Such differences in treatment are due to the insulation of the independent regulatory agencies from presidential politics and the deferential judicial standards of review that they enjoy. In contrast, cabinet agencies are closely tied to the partisan politics of the White House. A dichotomous variable is used to denote cabinet agencies (1 = cabinet agencies, 0 = independent regulatory agencies and non-cabinet foreign/ military affairs policy agencies). This variable is used to test the hypothesis that the proximity of the agency to the president and White House politics is negatively associated with the likelihood that a justice will vote in favor of the agency.

PETITIONER STATUS. This is a dichotomous variable denoting the status of the agency in the appeal as either the petitioner (party appealing the case to the Supreme Court, coded 1) or as the respondent (party responding to an appeal to the Supreme Court, coded 0). The distinction between petitioner and respondent status is an important one because, as mentioned earlier, the Court ordinarily is inclined to accept cases for review that it wishes to reverse (e.g., Segal and Spaeth 1993, Kearney and Sheehan 1992). Further, given the tremendous amount of discretion that the executive branch has in determining which agency cases are appealed to the Court, it is plausible that agencies typically only appear as petitioners when they have a highly meritorious claim (e.g., Devins 1994). Thus, it is expected that agencies will do better when they appear before the Court as petitioners rather than as respondents.

PRESIDENTIAL APPROVAL AND PROXIMITY. As previously noted, the cabinet agencies are often associated with high-profile political appointments and partisan-based policy initiatives. As opposed to the independent regulatory agencies, cabinet agencies are more closely affiliated with the president and White House politics. Given the above, it is tenable that the success of cabinet agencies before the Court might be particularly coterminous with presidential prestige. Therefore, I hypothesized further that the influence of presidential approval should matter more in those cases concerning the agencies closest to the president and White House politics, the cabinet agencies. An interactive term is used to test the effects of presidential approval on the success of the cabinet agencies specifically (cabinet agency multiplied by presidential approval), with all agencies other than cabinet agencies (independent regulatory agencies and non-cabinet foreign/military affairs policy agencies) compared as the reference category.

Last, dummy variables for presidential administrations are included, with Eisenhower's administration (the most predominant in the data set) left out of the equation as the reference category. As previously noted, these variables are necessary to control for interadministration fluctuations that may occur due to characteristics and phenomena attributable to specific presidents.

Results

The model's results are displayed in table 5. Overall, the model has fairly modest predictive capability with a 12% reduction in predictive error, no doubt partially due to a somewhat skewed dependent variable (66% in modal category). However, the formal goodness-of-fit test (chi square) indicates that the model is sufficient for explanation.

The M.L.E. coefficients indicate the change in the log of the odds ratio for a vote in favor of an agency, while holding the other variables constant. The final column in the table, Impact, represents the change in the probability that a justice will vote in favor of an agency given the noted changes in the variable in question, while holding the other independent variables at their mean/modal values.

The influence of presidential prestige (public approval) on justice voting can be assessed by examining the coefficients for the base variable Presidential Approval along with the interaction term Presidential Approval—Agency Proximity. The Presidential Approval variable is a reference category, and its coefficient

Table 5. Logistic Regression Model for the Likelihood that Justices Will Vote in Favor of Agencies

Variable	M. L. E.	S. E.	Impact[a]
Foreign/Military Affairs Agency	.1844*	.1062	5%
Judicial Appointment	.2291**	.0892	6%
Same Party	–.0742	.0717	—
Executive Experience	.1182*	.0664	3%
Agency Decision Liberal	.5374**	.0677	See Fig. 8
Justice Ideology	–.8522**	.0665	See Fig. 8[b]
Agency Decision Liberal × Justice Ideology	1.4987**	.0925	See Fig. 8
Agency Proximity	–1.1780**	.3270	See Fig. 9
Presidential Approval	–.0053	.0044	See Fig. 9
Presidential Approval × Agency Proximity	.0229**	.0060	See Fig. 9[c]
Agency Petitioner	.3913**	.0624	10%
Kennedy	.1830	.1446	—
Johnson	.6008	.1327	—
Nixon	.1182	.1213	—
Ford	.4445	.1737	—
Carter	.4810	.1404	—
Reagan	.6452	.1187	—

(continued)

Table 5. Logistic Regression Model for the Likelihood that Justices Will Vote in Favor of Agencies *(continued)*

Variable	M. L. E.	S. E.	Impact[a]
Bush	.2889	.1579	—
Clinton	.3352	.2113	—
Intercept	.0216	.3065	—

M. L. E. = maximum likelihood estimate; S. E. = standard error
Model chi square = 607.16, df = 19, P < .001
–2 × LLR = 6619.44
% correctly predicted = 69.84%
Null = 65.7%
Reduction in error = 12%
N = 5617

*Significant at .05

**Significant at .01

[a]The impact value displayed is the impact on the probability of a pro-agency vote for a one unit change in the value of dichotomous variables and a one standard-deviation change in the value of continuous variables while holding all other variables at their mean/modal values.

[b]The Segal, et al. (1995) measure for justice ideology ranges from –1 to +1 and has a mean of .10. A one standard deviation change in the measure is .67.

[c]The presidential approval measure ranges from 35 to 76 and has a mean of 54.7. A one standard deviation change in the measure is 11.3.

represents the effect of presidential approval on justice voting in those cases involving non-cabinet foreign policy agencies and independent regulatory agencies. It does not attain statistical significance. The coefficient for the interaction term (Presidential Approval—Agency Proximity) is in the predicted direction and is statistically significant. The impact estimate (see figure 9) demonstrates that presidential approval exerts a moderate influence on justice voting in the typical situation (a one standard deviation change in presidential approval). With larger fluctions of presidential approval, its influence is more substantial.[22] Thus,

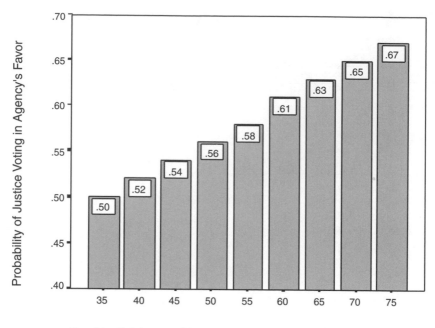

Presidential Approval Level

**Figure 9. The Effect of Presidential Approval
on Justice Voting in Cabinet Agency Cases**

presidential prestige matters where theory predicts that it would
be more pervasive; in the agencies most closely tied to White
House politics (the cabinet agencies).[23] Also, the Agency Proximity variable coefficient indicates that the president's cabinet agencies fare poorly (compared to independent regulatory agencies
and non-cabinet foreign policy agencies) when presidential approval is low.

It is important to note the conditional relationship that the
coefficient for this variable (Agency Proximity) represents. The
coefficient indicates the effect of agency proximity (the presence
of a cabinet agency before the Court) when presidential approval
is at zero. While this is theoretically a possible reality, such an
instance does not actually occur in the data set. Auxiliary regressions were employed to further examine this conditional relationship. The Presidential Approval variable was calibrated so
that the coefficient would represent the conditional relationship

in question at varying actual observed levels of presidential approval (See Friedrich 1982, Smith and Sasaki 1979). Indeed, it was found that at low levels of observed presidential approval, agencies' proximity to the president was associated with a lower likelihood of favorable voting by justices. Further, at high levels of actually observed presidential approval, agency proximity to the president was associated with a higher likelihood of favorable voting by justices. Cross-tabulation analysis reveals that as a general proposition there appears to be little distinction in the justices' treatment of cabinet agencies and independent regulatory agencies. Cabinet agencies received 66% favorable votes compared to 67% favorable votes for independent regulatory agencies. Auxilliary regressions run without the presidential approval interaction terms reveal no statistically significant difference between the likelihood of favorable voting for independent regulatory agencies and cabinet agencies.

Wildavsky's (1966) two presidencies thesis is supported by the statistically significant coefficient for the Foreign/Military Affairs Agency variable. Thus, the president, via his bureaucratic arm, receives more deference from the Court in the foreign policy sphere than in the domestic arena. This model also yields political and background variables that are found to be statistically significant determinants of agency success with the Supreme Court justices. First, the coefficient for Judicial Appointment shows that justices are, to a certain degree, politically loyal in that they are more likely to vote in favor of the president's bureaucracy when they were appointed by the president in office. Second, the coefficient for Executive Experience indicates that justices with executive branch backgrounds are likely to be sympathetic towards the federal agencies. The impact estimates for these three variables (Foreign/Military Affairs Agency, Judicial Appointment, and Executive Experience) are modest, indicating that such factors are likely to influence justices' votes only at the margins.

Consistent with Segal and Spaeth (1993) and Sheehan (1990, 1992), judicial ideology is very useful in explaining justices' voting on agency cases. The coefficient for the reference variable Justice Ideology indicates that when an agency brings a conservative case to the Court, the likelihood of a justice voting for the agency is inversely related to the justice's ideology score. In other words, the more liberal the justice, the more likely that he or she will vote against an agencies' conservative litigation position. Similarly, the coefficient for the interaction term Agency Decision Liberal × Justice Ideology indicates that more liberal justices are more likely to vote in favor of an agency when the agency takes a liberal litigation stance (i.e., defending a previous liberal agency decision). The coefficient for the reference category Agency Decision Liberal indicates that when agencies bring liberal cases to Court, they can expect favorable votes from what might be considered "moderate" justices' (i.e., the effect of agency ideological direction when justice ideology is at zero). Clearly, the findings here show that attitudes matter in justice voting on agency cases. In fact, the impact estimates (see figure 10) reveal that justice ideology is perhaps the most influential factor in justices' voting on agency cases. However, while the impact of attitudes on justice voting is substantial, this model demonstrates

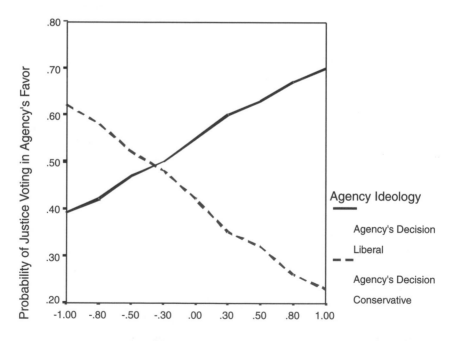

Jusice Ideology: Conservative (-) Liberal (+)

Figure 10. The Effect of Justice Ideology on Voting for Agencies by Agency Decision Ideological Direction

that factors other than attitudes can have a statistically significant impact on justice voting.[24]

Finally, the coefficient for the variable Agency Petitioner indicates that the president's agencies are likely to be more successful in Supreme Court litigation when they appear as petitioners rather than as respondents. This finding suggests that there may be underlying selection effects involved in agency litigation before the Supreme Court.

Possible Selection Effects

Some scholars argue that the executive branch (i.e., the Department of Justice and the solicitor general)[25] is strategic in the selection of agency cases that it appeals to the Supreme Court (e.g., Devins 1994, Zorn 2001, 1997a, 1997b). It is possible that a variety of factors, including perceived potential success, importance, and cost of the case to the executive branch, may influence the decision to appeal a lower court agency loss.

Essentially, the Court cannot hear a case that the executive branch decides not to appeal. Therefore, in its decision to appeal a case to the Court the executive branch may be able to affect how its agencies are treated by the Court. It should also be reiterated that the Court has tremendous discretion with regard to its docket in agency cases (as opposed to cases that involve the president's formal powers). Thus, the general rule of thumb that the Court takes on cases to reverse them in favor of petitioners (Provine 1980), is applicable in this litigation situation.

When an agency comes before the Court as a litigator the strategic selection considerations that may have been involved in getting it there are, in a word, complex. Figure 11 details the intricate selection process that may bring an agency before the Court as a litigator. As the figure demonstrates, whether an agency appears before the Court as a petitioner or as a respondent can be influenced by the decision processes of the lower court, the executive branch, litigation opponents, and the Supreme Court.

In order to assess whether a selection effect may be at work in the justices' decisions on these cases, auxiliary logistic regressions were performed to help explain the likelihood that agencies would appear before the Court as petitioners rather than as respondents. The Heckman (1979) procedure, outlined in chapter 3, is

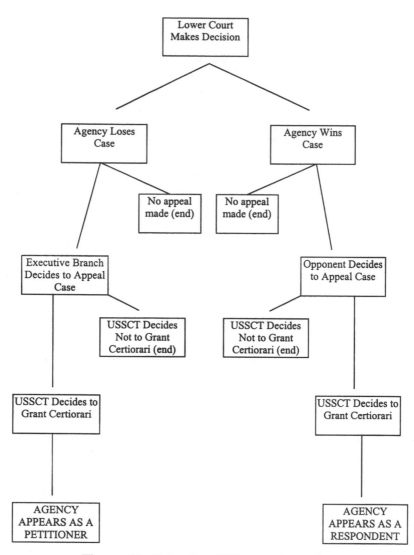

Figure 11. Selection Effects—Agencies

again followed. The results of these auxiliary regressions are presented in table 6. In the Step One Regression, it was found that agencies were more likely to appear as petitioners: 1) where the ideological direction of the agency decision was closer to the ideological composition of the Court;[26] 2) where the case was important to the executive branch;[27] and 3) when the president was experiencing high public approval.[28] Again, as in chapter 3, I find that presidential approval has a statistically significant effect on the likelihood that the executive branch (agencies here) will appear before the Court as a petitioner. Thus, when the president is enjoying high popularity his bureaucratic litigation delegates (the Department of Justice and the solicitor general) are likely to feel more confident in how the executive branch will be treated by the Supreme Court justices.

However, in the Step Two Regression[29] the statistically insignificant Predicted Probabilities variable provides no evidence of a strategic selection influence on voting outcomes. In other words, any strategy that may be employed by the executive branch appears to yield no discernable dividends concerning the justices' voting once the case gets to the Supreme Court. However, it is important to reiterate that the selection model employed here is somewhat rudimentary, especially given the extremely complex process set forth in figure 11. Consequently, these results should be regarded as exploratory in nature. Zorn (2001, 1997a, 1997b) makes a compelling case that the executive branch acts strategically in its selection of agency cases to appeal to the Supreme Court. The results here indicate that agencies fare much better before the Court when they appear by choice as petitioners, rather than being haled before the Court as respondents where they have less opportunity for case selection strategy. While competing explanations for the impact of agency litigation status on agency success before the Court are viable (e.g., Court certiorari discretion), these results tend to suggest that agency success before the Court may be at least partially attributable to a careful selection process undertaken by the executive branch.

Discussion

This chapter's examination of the federal agencies before the Court provides insight into one aspect of the multifaceted and complex relationship that exists between the president and the Supreme Court. It also provides beneficial insight concerning the viability of a "presidentialized" bureaucracy.

Moe (1998) argues that the president has the upper hand on Congress in bureaucratic politics. He asserts, "however much

Table 6. Agency Selection Effects—
First and Second Step Logistic Regression Results

Step One Regression—The Likelihood that an Agency will Appear as Petitioner			Step Two Regression—The Likelihood that a Justice will Vote for an Agency		
Step One Variables	M. L. E.	S. E.	Step Two Variables	M. L. E.	S. E.
Agency Decision Liberal (ADL)	−.2236**	.0704	Agency Decision Liberal (ADL)	.5259**	.0886
Court Agenda (CA)	−3.1344**	.3791	Justice Ideology (JI)	−.8204**	.0842
ADL × CA	3.0321**	.1881	ADL × JI	1.2427**	.1273
Criminal Procedure	−.9340**	.2131	President Appointment	.2136*	.1154
Civil Rights & Liberties	−.6920**	.0849	Executive Experience	.0904	.0848
Labor	−.4285**	.0773	Same Party	.0774	.0920
Constit. Law Issues	.2919**	.1034	Foreign Agency	.4477**	.1246
President Approval (lag 1 yr)	.0059*	.0031	President Approval (PA)	−.0195**	.0056
Intercept	1.2221**	.2679	Proximity (P)	−1.721**	.4160
—	—	—	PA × P	.0339**	.0077
					(continued)

**Table 6. Agency Selection Effects—
First and Second Step Logistic Regression Results** *(continued)*

Step One Regression—The Likelihood an Agency will Appear as Petitioner			Step Two Regression—The Likelihood that a Justice will Vote for an Agency		
Step One Variables	M. L. E.	S. E.	Step Two Variables	M. L. E.	S. E.
—	—	—	Predicted Probs.	.3535	.3544
—	—	—	Intercept	.9485*	.4288

M.L.E. = maximum likelihood estimate
S.E. = standard error

Note: Presidential Dummy
Variables are not displayed.

Chi square = 508.46 P < .01
Reduction in error = 11.93%
N = 5617

*Significant at .05

**Significant at .01

M.L.E. = maximum likelihood estimate
S.E. = standard error

Note: Presidential Dummy
Variables are not displayed.

Chi square = 328.52 P < .01
Reduction in error = 9.46%
N = 3604

*Significant at .05

**Significant at .01

Congress tries to structure things, the president can use his own institution's—and through it, the agencies'—informational and operational advantages to promote the presidential agenda" (444). Thus, presidents can politicize the bureaucracy toward their policy goals against a relatively structurally weak legislative branch (Moe and Wilson 1994). However, legal scholars are quick to point out that Congress is not the only other branch of the federal government and that the Supreme Court may play an important role in monitoring presidential efforts to assert political control over the bureaucracy (e.g., Romano 1994). Indeed, under our constitutional system of separation of powers, the Court stands as one of the primary formal checks on presidential bureaucratic power. However, the results presented here demonstrate that the Court justices are generally deferential toward agency action and thus, operate more as facilitators of presidential bureaucratic power (see figure 6). Additionally, the hypotheses tested here indicate that certain attitudinal, political, and external factors can influence the likelihood that the justices will act as checks or facilitators of presidential power through the federal agencies. These results suggest possible avenues for executive strategy in bureaucratic Supreme Court litigation.

The power of appointment is certainly an effective strategy if available to a president. The results presented here show that justices tend to support the bureaucratic agents of the presidents who appointed them. Further, the appointment power permits the president to alter, to some degree, the ideological composition of the Court. Consistent with Sheehan (1990, 1992), I find that the ideological direction of the agency's prior decision, coupled with justice ideology, helps to explain justices' voting outcomes. In other words, liberal justices are more apt to favor liberal agency actions and conservative justices are more likely to favor conservative agency policy decisions. Further, justices with prior executive experience are generally more supportive of bureaucratic actions. Thus, presidents may be well advised to consider this factor in their appointment decisions.

The executive branch may also promote its own cause through the cases it selects for litigation. The litigation status variable indicates that agencies fare better when they are appearing before the Court as petitioners rather than as respondents. Thus, a careful appeal strategy may be politically advantageous to the executive office. Further, the two presidencies thesis finds support in this study. Agencies that implement presidential foreign policy tend to receive more deference from the justices than agencies that implement domestic policy. All of this suggests that presidents may be able to improve their lot before the Court through careful selection of which disputes to appeal to the Court. As noted in chapter 3, it may be more prudent in certain circumstances to let a lower court loss stand than to risk setting precedent that is authoritative and anti-bureaucracy by appealing to the Supreme Court.

Last, we see that presidential prestige affects justice decision making when the president's cabinet agencies come before the Court. These are the agencies that are most closely tied to the president and his partisan administrative policies. Thus, it is perhaps not too surprising that their Court success might also be

tied to the public prestige possessed by the president. This finding indicates that presidential prestige may work as political capital for the president in bureaucratic litigation before the Court.

The president's political power (success) before the Court
can now be assessed both directly (formal powers of office) and
via his bureaucratic agents. In chapter 3 the results indicate that
the degree of deference from the justices that the president
receives (with regard to his formal powers of office) may turn on
factors such as the justices' attitudes, the type of power at issue
(foreign versus domestic), whether he appointed the justice, and
his relative standing in the polls. In this chapter, I find that such
factors may also influence the degree to which justices defer to
the president's bureaucratic agents. In sum, the general theories
posited in chapter 2 appear to work well as predictors of presidential fortunes both when he appears directly, litigating the
formal powers of the executive office, and when his bureaucratic
agents appear before the Court to litigate executive policy. Notably, the president's public prestige factors into his success as a
litigant in both the formal power and bureaucratic power contexts. In the next chapter, I assess whether the president can
extend this use of his public prestige to influence Court outcomes in cases in which he does not appear directly before the
court or through his bureaucratic agencies, but rather has publicly expressed an interest in the direction of American legal
policy.

Chapter Five

Presidential Policy Signals and Supreme Court Justice Decision Making

Examining the Bounds of Presidential Influence on Justice Policy Voting

George C. Edwards suggests that "the presidency is perhaps the most important and least understood policy making institution in the United States" (ix 1985). Indeed, the extant literature on presidential political power suggests that the presidency is an influential institution in national policy-making and implementation (e.g., Edwards and Wayne 1994). If we assume that presidents wish to effectively advance their policy preferences, then it is important to discern the parameters and determinants of presidential policy influence. For the presidency to function effectively as a policy-making institution it must gain the support or acquiescence of other important political actors (Edwards 1985). This ability to gain policy support can be likened to Neustadt's assertion that the policy-making power of the presidency is essentially the power to persuade.

To date, there have been numerous assessments of the ability of the president to influence other relevant political actors, including the president's influence in Congressional policy-making (e.g., Edwards 1980, Rivers and Rose 1985, Bond and Fleisher 1990, Sullivan 1991, Brace and Hinckley 1992) and presidential influence on public attitudes concerning policy priorities (Cohen 1993, 1995), among others. Of course, the president's policy agenda often includes issues that involve the federal courts in litigation situations (e.g., civil rights), thus, making the federal judiciary a relevant player in executive policy-making.

However, while judicial scholars have quantitatively assessed the presidents' ability to influence federal district court policy-making through the appointment process (e.g., Stidham and Carp 1987) and some assessments of presidential policy influence via appointment exist concerning the Supreme Court (e.g., Abraham 1992, Goldman 1989), there remains a paucity of quantitative analysis on the president's ability to influence the policy-making of the Supreme Court outside of the appointment process.

While studies concerning Supreme Court appointment assess the president's ability to place "like-minded" judicial actors on the Court, they provide little information as to the president's ability to contemporaneously influence the policy-making of the justices already sitting on the Court. The Supreme Court ultimately acts as the policy leader in federal judicial policy-making since its opinions set the precedent that the lower courts follow. Thus, the president's ability to get his policy preferences implemented in certain policy areas is, to an extent, conditioned upon the degree to which the Supreme Court is willing to comply.

A review of the literature indicates that attempts by the president to directly influence Court decision making, through private communications with the Court, have been rare and largely unsuccessful (e.g., Edwards and Wayne 1985). In this study I do not examine such private attempts to influence the Supreme Court. I instead look at the presidents' attempts to influence the Supreme Court by using public signals of their policy preferences (Kernell 1986, Edwards 1983). Specifically, I endeavor to ascertain whether presidents' publicly expressed policy-preference signals are heeded by the Supreme Court justices and whether they are responsive to presidential prestige (public approval) in their choice to support or not support presidents' demonstrated policy preferences.

Research Design

The premise that presidents can get their policy preferences supported by the Supreme Court by sending overt policy signals suggests that Supreme Court justices reference external factors in deciding cases. It might be argued that any relationship between presidential policy preferences and Supreme Court justice decision making is indirect through the appointment process. This theory dictates that presidents appoint candidates who share their policy inclinations and, once confirmed, those appointees simply follow their sincere ideological preferences in voting. Proponents of this view note that Supreme Court justices are appointed for life and have no further progressive ambitions, since they have reached the pinnacle of the federal judiciary. Thus, justices should not be responsive to external influences and such factors are not responsible for any congruence that may exist between presidential policy preferences and Court decision making (Norpoth and Segal 1994, Segal and Spaeth 1993). This study seeks to discern whether presidential attempts to publicly signal their policy preferences affect justices' decision making while holding their ideological inclinations constant.

In the first section of this chapter I address whether presidential attempts to "go public" with rhetorical signals can affect Supreme Court policy-making. However, public rhetoric is not the only manner in which the president can send overt policy signals. In the second portion of this chapter I address the executive's ability to influence Court policy-making by sending policy signals through his primary legal arm, the solicitor general.

Dependent Variable

This chapter first examines the propensity of the Supreme Court justices to choose to promote a policy that presidents have sent rhetorical signals in favor of promoting. I look at four separate policy areas that the Court has regularly ruled on and which have typically been a part of the president's policy agenda: law and order, civil rights, labor rights, and foreign policy.

Labor and management disputes and general employee issues have been a regular (and often contentious) topic for Supreme Court review. Similarly, civil rights and law and order policy issues have been frequent areas of Supreme Court policy-making (see generally, Segal and Spaeth 1993). Foreign policy issues have not been as much of a staple of Supreme Court litigation over the years, however, foreign policy issues have led to some of the best-known president-Court interactions in history (see Witt 1990). Further, examination of foreign policy issues provides an opportunity to assess the two presidencies thesis with regard to the impact of presidential rhetoric on justice decision making. The issues examined here also customarily occupy presidents' policy attention (e.g., Light 1991).

The Supreme Court cases examined here cover the years 1953 to 1995, and the data on them are derived from the *United States Supreme Court Judicial Database* (ICPSR 9422). The policy area of Law and Order includes justices' votes on cases before the Court that involve the rights of persons accused of crimes and related issues. The policy area of Civil Rights encompasses votes on non-First Amendment freedom cases, which pertain to classifications based on race, age, indigency, voting, residency, military or handicapped status, gender, and alienage. The policy area of Labor Rights includes votes on cases concerning the rights of employees and employee unions. Finally, the policy area of Foreign Policy includes votes on cases that deal with issues such as immigration, war crimes, alienage, the military, the draft, loyalty, and security risks (see Spaeth—*Supreme Court Judicial Database Codebook* ICPSR 9422). Each of these votes is coded on a policy-outcome dimension so as to denote the policy directionality of the justice's decision. Law and order cases are coded 1 if the justice's vote promotes law and order (i.e., goes against a person accused of or convicted of a crime). Votes that are pro-defendant, on the other hand, are coded 0. Civil rights cases are coded 1 if the justice's decision promotes the interests of civil rights claimants. Votes going against civil rights claimants are coded 0. Labor rights votes are coded 1 if they promote the interests of labor unions or employees generally (e.g., a decision promoting the Occupational Safety and Health Act). Votes going against labor unions and employees are coded 0. Finally, foreign policy votes are also coded on a liberal-conservative dimension. For example, justices' votes that favor aliens, immigrants, war crime defendants, and conscientious objectors are coded 1 (liberal), and votes going against these interests are coded 0 (conservative). Further, the foreign policy area is subdivided into issues dealing with matters of diplomacy (e.g., immigration) and matters relating to defense policy (e.g., conscientious objectors).

Hypotheses and Independent Variables

In order to help explain the justices' decisions to vote in favor of or against the policies described above, I provide independent variables based on the theories of judicial decision making outlined below. These variables test competing explanations of judicial decision making on the policies outlined above.

PRESIDENTIAL POLICY SIGNALS. In order to determine whether a relationship exists between presidential policy preferences and justice policy-making outcomes, it is necessary to discern what presidents' policy preferences are. This has typically proven to be a problematic endeavor for judicial scholars since, as opposed to legislative presidential preferences, no standard measure for presidential "judicial policy preferences" exists. Stidham and Carp (1987), in their study on presidential policy preferences and federal district court policy outcomes, utilized anecdotal evidence and references from party presidential election platforms to discern the policy preferences of Presidents Carter and Reagan. Alternatively, Link (1995) and Mishler and Sheehan (1993) used a simple partisan dummy variable to measure presidents' policy preferences, assuming that Democratic presidents were uniformly liberal and that Republican presidents were uniformly conservative in their policy preferences. While these methods of assessing presidential policy preferences are reasonable, I attempt to provide perhaps a more exacting measure of the policy predilections of presidents. I discern presidents' policy preferences by examining their treatment of these policy issue areas in their annual State of the Union addresses.

The State of the Union address is basically the president's annual public statement of his administration's policy plan. In *The President's Agenda*, Paul Light asserts that the State of the Union addresses are the primary indicators of presidential policy priorities. He notes that, "the recent history of the State of the Union address certainly reinforces its value as a priority-setting device. At least since Theodore Roosevelt, presidents have used the message as a statement of both foreign and domestic priorities" (Light 1991, 160; see also Cohen 1997, on the use of State of the Union addresses as indicators of presidential policy priorities).

Hence, from these high-profile public addresses we can determine whether a policy was deemed important enough for inclusion on the president's State of the Union policy agenda and, further, what his substantive policy preference was (e.g., pro-law and order as opposed to pro-rights-of-accused-citizens). Thus, the presidents' State of the Union addresses are analyzed in order to determine the presidents' stances and priorities on these issues (civil rights, law and order, labor rights, and foreign policy).

If a president places particular emphasis on a policy area by emphasizing it in his State of the Union address, this is an indication that the president is sending a public signal that this policy preference is one of importance and should be carefully considered by the other branches of government and the public at large (i.e., "going public": see generally, Light 1991, Kernell 1986, Cohen 1993, 1995, 1997). Favorable mention in the State of the Union address gives a policy both visibility and presidential support (Cohen 1997). At bottom line, the president is spending valuable time in the public eye and political capital to promote the policy.

While Cohen (1993, 1995) has made a convincing case that such presidential signaling (i.e., State of the Union addresses) can affect public opinion on policy issues, support for the premise that presidential rhetoric can influence the behavior of elite political actors seems less clear. Several scholars assert that presidential rhetoric can have a powerful influence on both the public and on elite political actors (e.g., Hart 1987, Medhurst 1993, Smith and Smith 1994). However, Edwards (1996) argues that such assertions are often based on unreliable (or no) empirical evidence, and that the notion the president can influence elite political actors through rhetoric is much more attenuated and complex than the commanding "bully pulpit" figure that some presidential scholars suggest. However, if the Court justices do reference presidential policy concerns, then such rhetorical signaling may have an impact on decisions.

Here, presidential policy preference signals are estimated by analyzing presidents' public statements in their State of the Union addresses for each year studied (1953–95). The coding strategy is generally consistent with that used in previous work on the State of the Union address (see Cohen 1993, 1995, 1997,

Kessler 1974). The number of lines in a president's State of the Union address are calculated for each of the four policy areas examined. A policy direction is then assigned to the statement based on its substantive ideological inclination. Analysis of presidents' State of the Union addresses allows me to assess both the direction and magnitude of presidential preferences on specific policy areas. Thus, I am concerned not only with the presidents' policy preferences (i.e., ideological direction), I am also concerned with the level of priority or emphasis that the president places on those policy preferences (i.e., preference magnitude).

Presidential policy preference signals are measured by assessing the balance of the directionality of the president's statements. The variable Presidential Preference Signals denotes the president's relative promotion (or lack thereof) of a given policy in his State of the Union address. For example, if in a president's State of the Union address a president discusses the need for crime control and spends fifty lines of copy on this topic, then the president's "score" for supporting law and order in that year is fifty lines divided by the total number of lines contained in that State of the Union address.[30]

It is not uncommon for presidents to provide conflicting statements on a given policy. This may occur due to political posturing by the president, or perhaps may be the result of sincerely discordant policy preferences. For example, presidents may want law and order while still caring about the rights of accused citizens—ostensibly, conflicting objectives. This variable takes into account such discrepant rhetoric by using the balance of the president's statements to obtain what might be considered the president's "net policy stance" in this situation. For instance, if in the hypothetical law and order situation described above, the president spent fifty lines stressing the need to get tough on crime and only ten lines emphasizing the rights of the criminally accused, then the president's preference or promotion of this policy for that year would be forty lines pro-law-and-order.[31]

Figure 12 shows the degree to which presidents have emphasized Labor Rights, Civil Rights, and Law and Order in their State of the Union addresses during the time period studied.[32] These policy areas have been described by Cohen (1997) as being "discretionary," meaning that they compete for space on the State of the Union address after "required" policy areas have been

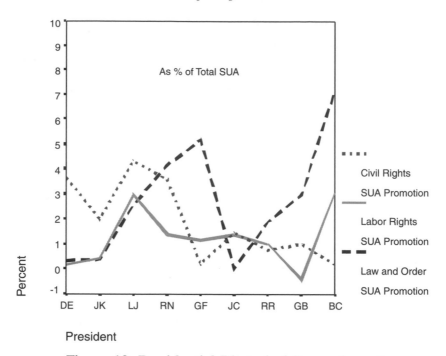

As % of Total SUA

Civil Rights
SUA Promotion

Labor Rights
SUA Promotion

Law and Order
SUA Promotion

President

**Figure 12. Presidential Rhetorical Promotion of
Civil Rights, Law and Order, and Labor Rights in
State of the Union Addresses**

covered. Cohen explains that foreign policy and the economy
(e.g., budgeting, inflation, etc.) are the two primary policies that
are permanently on the agenda—"required" parts the State of
the Union Address. He notes that, "The difference between required and discretionary policies is that required ones always
reach the top of the public's policy agenda, and they affect large
numbers of people in significant ways. Discretionary policies or
issues are less able to hold public concern and attention for long
periods of time" (1997, 40). Thus, while still important to the
president, these policy areas typically comprise a smaller portion
of the State of the Union address than required policy areas.

Figure 10 reveals that civil rights rhetoric has fluctuated by
administration, however there is a decided decline since the Nixon
administration. In the post-Nixon era, presidents—both Republican and Democrat—have placed lower priority on civil rights

concerns in their primary annual public address. However, civil rights by no means faded from the presidential rhetorical agenda. President Jimmy Carter stressed his administration's commitment to equal opportunity in his 1978 State of the Union message, asserting: "A major priority for our nation is the final elimination of barriers that restrict the opportunities available to women, and to black people, Hispanics and other minorities. We have come a long way toward that goal, but there is still much to do. What we inherited from the past must not be permitted to shackle us in the future."

In law and order policy, rhetoric experienced a sharp incline from the Eisenhower administration through the Ford administration, was ignored by Carter, and then experienced another sharp increase thereafter under the Reagan and Bush administrations, with Clinton continuing the emphasis on crime control. Ronald Reagan's 1982 call for tough law and order policy is indicative of this trend: "So, too, the problem of crime—one as real and deadly serious as any in America today—demands that we seek transformation of our legal system, which overly protects the rights of criminals while it leaves society and the innocent victims of crime without justice."

Presidential promotion of labor rights received sparse attention from presidents Eisenhower and Kennedy, but Johnson placed particular emphasis on promoting labor. In his 1966 message he vowed to strengthen worker rights and well-being, stating: "For those who labor, I propose to improve unemployment insurance, to expand minimum wage benefits, and by the repeal of section 14(b) of the Taft-Hartley Act to make the labor laws in all our states equal to the laws of the 31 states which do not have right-to-work measures." Presidential attention to labor rights has generally decreased since Johnson, but experienced an upward turn during the early years of Clinton's presidency.

Figure 13 shows the degree to which presidents have emphasized their policy positions in the State of the Union addresses on Defense Policy and Diplomacy Policy. As noted earlier, foreign policy is a required policy area that typically takes up a large portion of the president's address relative to discretionary policies. However, as indicated in figure 11, the two subcategories (defense and diplomacy) are not equal in this regard. Presidents generally spend considerably less time on foreign diplomacy

Popular Justice

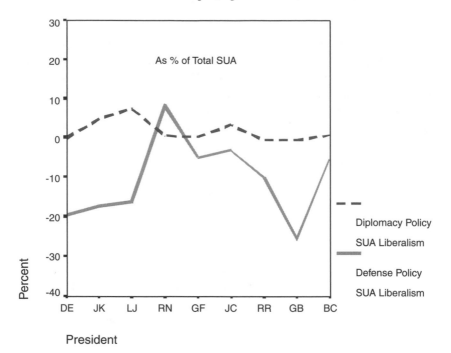

**Figure 13. Presidential Rhetorical Liberalism in State
of the Union Addresses: Foreign Diplomacy Policy
and Foreign Defense Policy**

policy issues such as immigration, peace talks (as third party),
and foreign aid than they do on defense policy.

Presidents are consistently conservative in their defense
policy rhetoric, on balance, with the exception of Richard Nixon.
While Nixon was not reluctant to make conservative statements
with regard to defense policy (e.g., support for the military), on
balance his rhetoric leaned heavily toward more liberal propositions. In addition to advocating a general strategy of non-inter-
vention, Nixon changed the presidential tenor of relations with
the major communist powers. In his 1974 address, he asserted:
"In our relations with the Soviet Union, we have turned away
from a policy of confrontation to one of negotiation. For the first
time since World War II, the world's two strongest powers are
working together towards peace in the world. With the People's
Republic of China after a generation of hostile isolation, we have
begun a period of peaceful exchange and expanding trade." The

most conservative defense policy president was George Bush, who spent over 25 percent of his State of the Union addresses on conservative defense-policy rhetoric, much of which came in the address following the conclusion of the popular Persian Gulf War.

Given that the State of the Union address is a credible indicator of presidential agendas (Light 1991), the variation in presidents' promotion of the policies outlined above in their State of the Union addresses provides useful insight into administration policy priorities. In short, presidents use the State of the Union address to send clear public signals as to which policies are important to them. This variable is used to test the hypothesis that justices heed presidential policy concerns and are influenced by presidential policy rhetoric.

PRESIDENTIAL PRESTIGE. The president's ability to go public with regard to congressional policy-making has been found to be conditioned upon the president's popular prestige (public approval rating; e.g., Rivers and Rose 1985, Brace and Hinckley 1992). In this model I extend the theory that a president's ability to influence other political actors—e.g., to the policy-making of the Supreme Court justices—is conditioned by his popular support.

Presidential prestige is assessed by using as a base variable the annual average of the Gallup presidential approval polls for each of the forty-three years in which these Court decisions occur (see figure 8). This annual mean level of the president's approval is then multiplied by the president's policy preference signal variable to produce an interactive variable that measures both the direction and extent of a president's preferences along with his level of public support.

This variable taps into the notion that a president with majoritarian public support behind him will have greater persuasive power with other political actors (e.g., Edwards 1980, Neustadt 1990). It is used to assess the hypothesis that the Court justices are influenced by the level of presidential prestige in their voting decisions on whether or not to follow a president's publicly proclaimed policy preferences. It is anticipated that the justices are more likely to support a president's policy preferences when he enjoys strong public backing.

JUSTICE IDEOLOGY. As outlined in depth in chapter 2, it is important to consider the effects of justices' personal attitudes on their voting behavior. Here, I again use the ideology scores developed by Segal and others (1989, 1995) to assess the impact of justices' personal ideological inclinations on their propensity to vote for or against a given policy.

COURT AGENDA. It is also important to consider the possibility that legal agenda effects may influence justice policy decision making, as has been noted by several judicial scholars (e.g., Baum 1988, 1992, Link 1995, Mishler and Sheehan 1993, 1996, Flemming and Wood 1997). The concept of agenda effects denotes the possibility that the types of legal issues before the Court, as well as the ideological direction and intensity of those issues, may fluctuate over time. The inherent concern is that justices may appear to be more or less liberal or conservative over time, when in fact their attitudes remain the same. It is the Court's agenda that changes (Mishler and Sheehan 1996, 181).

To assess agenda effects I draw upon the general strategy suggested by Mishler and Sheehan (1996). They explain that the Court, for the most part, controls its own agenda through the certiorari process and that the Court's agenda is substantially analogous to the ideological balance of the Court itself. To account for agenda effects I include a measure of democratic control of the Court's agenda.[33] This is a dichotomous variable that is coded 1 when the majority of the justices on the Court are democrats, and coded 0 otherwise. It is anticipated that when the Court's ideological agenda (ideological balance) is more liberal (i.e., controlled by democrats), then it will be more difficult for justices to cast liberal votes (and vice versa).

LITIGATION STATUS. The Supreme Court generally takes on for review cases that it wishes to overturn (Segal and Spaeth 1993)[34], therefore the party appearing before the Court as a petitioner is more likely to win than a respondent, given this general norm of Court behavior. Thus, it is sensible that a justice would be more likely to vote for a litigant arguing a policy position before the Court (e.g., law and order) when that party's litigation status is as a petitioner. This variable is dichotomous (petitioner = 1, respondent = 0) and is used to test the hypothesis that the likelihood that a justice will vote to support a policy is positively related to whether that policy is being advanced by the petitioner in the case rather than the respondent.

Finally, dummy variables for presidential administrations are included with the most predominant administration left out of the equation as the reference category.[35] As previously noted, these variables are necessary to control for interadministration fluctuations that may occur due to characteristics and phenomena attributable to specific presidents.

Estimation and Results

In this model the dependent variable is, again, dichotomous and, hence, I use logistic regression for estimation. The specification outlined above is applied to each of the previously mentioned issue areas. Prior studies suggest that we might expect the impact of certain external influences on justice decision making to be contingent upon the type of issue area being assessed. Wildavsky (1966) and others have argued that the president enjoys more deference from other political actors in the area of foreign policy than in the area of domestic policy (the fabled two presidencies thesis). Hence, supporters of the two presidencies thesis might expect that the variable used here to measure presidential preferences (rhetoric) might be more influential in the foreign policy areas (diplomacy and defense policy) than in the domestic issue areas (civil rights, law and order, and labor rights).

With regard to differences among domestic issue areas, it is effectual to draw upon the general literature that examines the effect of external influences on justice voting. Flemming and Wood (1997) speculate that the effect of external influences (in their study, public mood) on justice voting may be contingent upon the saliency of the domestic issue area being assessed. They suggest that the more salient an issue area is, the more justice voting will be influenced by public mood. They find that public mood matters in civil rights, civil liberties, tax, and judicial power cases. However, they find no such effect in criminal procedure, labor, and economic cases. Compare this with the work of Link (1995), who finds that the Court is moved by public opinion in both criminal procedure and civil rights cases. He also finds however, that elite political actors' (president and congress) preferences only seem to matter in criminal procedure cases. He argues that the Court may consider itself a policy leader in certain issue areas (i.e., civil rights), and thus be less susceptible to the preferences of the other branches on these issues.

In sum, the literature on the influence of external influences on justice voting seems to suggest that certain domestic issue areas, i.e., the most salient, may be more susceptible to external influence, while issue areas in which the Court perceives itself as a leader may be less susceptible to such influences.

While the literature on the two presidencies thesis plainly suggests that presidential preferences should carry more weight in foreign policy issue cases, the literature concerning differences among domestic issue areas is less determinant.[36] In this chapter I am modeling the effect of external forces (presidential policy signals and presidential approval) on justice voting. Thus, the analysis presented here will provide a direct test of whether justices are susceptible to external influences in certain policy areas in which Court scholars believe that justices are resistant to such influence.[37]

The results of the logistic regression analyses on the issue areas Law and Order, Civil Rights, Labor Rights, Diplomacy, and Defense Policy are set forth in tables 7–12. The results of the model in each issue area may be compared by examining table 12, which provides a summary of model results. With regard to overall performance, the model is sufficient for explanation in each of the issue areas examined. However, the predictive capability of the model varies with the issue area being examined. The reduction of error calculations reveal that the model predicts best in the area of Law and Order (31% ROE [Reduction of Error]) and worst in the area of Labor Rights (2% ROE), where it is barely more helpful than the modal category.

Beyond the overall model results, the individual maximum-likelihood coefficients yield interesting information. Table 12 shows that the Presidential Policy Preferences (rhetoric) variable had the predicted effect in the issue areas of Civil Rights and Law and Order.[38] The variable had a counterintuitive effect in the issue area of Defense Policy, where there ostensibly exists a "backlash" voting effect by the justices when presidents publicly propound their ideological preferences on defense policy.

The issue area Law and Order, in which the president's ability to "go public" was found to be conditioned upon his public prestige, was where presidential popularity made justices more

Table 7. Presidential Policy Influence Model: Logistic Regression Results for Justices' Voting on Civil Rights Policy Cases

Variable	M. L. E.	S. E.	Impact[a]
Presidential Policy Signaling	.0388**	.0120	2.3%[b]
Presidential Approval (base)	−.0067	.0031	—
Presidential Policy Signaling × Presidential Approval	.0007	.0008	
Justice Ideology	.9693**	.0387	15.6%[c]
Court Agenda	−.0990	.1313	
Petitioner	.7227**	.0487	17.7%
Eisenhower	−.5586	.1248	—
Kennedy	.1436	.1712	—
Johnson	−.7267	.1683	—
Nixon	−.3902	.1557	—
Ford	−.2877	.0986	—
Carter	−.5279	.0826	—
Bush	.0945	.1034	—
Clinton	−.4029	.1251	—
Constant	.2273	.0525	—

M. L. E. = maximum likelihood estimate; S. E. = standard error
Model chi square = 1206.36, df = 14, P < .001
% correctly predicted = 65.97%
Null = 58.7%
Reduction in error = 17.6%
N = 8974

*Significant at .05

**Significant at .01

[a]The impact value displayed is the impact on the probability of a pro-civil rights vote for a one unit change in the value of dichotomous variables and a one standard deviation change in the value of continuous variables while holding all other variables at their mean/modal values.

[b]A one standard deviation change in the Presidential Policy Preferences measure is 2.41.

[c]A one standard deviation change in the Ideology measure is .69.

Table 8. Presidential Policy Influence Model: Logistic Regression Results for Justices' Voting on Law and Order Policy Cases

Variable	M. L. E.	S. E.	Impact[a]
Presidential Policy Signaling	.0161*	.0084	See Fig. 12[b]
Presidential Approval (base)	−.0033	.0027	See Fig. 12
Presidential Policy Signaling × Presidential Approval	.0079**	.0010	See Fig. 12[c]
Justice Ideology	−1.2021**	.0377	−20%[d]
Court Agenda	.0874	.0970	—
Petitioner	.8320**	.0471	16%
Eisenhower	.7231	.0951	—
Kennedy	.1867	.1431	—
Johnson	.5091	.1305	—
Nixon	.1697	.1238	—
Ford	.6260	.1116	—
Carter	−.1960	.0847	—
Bush	−.2187	.0843	—
Clinton	.4030	.1163	—
Constant	−.4063	.0540	—

M. L. E. = maximum likelihood estimate; S. E. = standard error
Model chi square = 1789.01, df = 14, P < .001
% correctly predicted = 66.87%
Null = 51.8%
Reduction in error = 31.3%
N = 10720

*Significant at .05

**Significant at .01

[a]The impact value displayed is the impact on the probability of a pro-law and order vote for a one unit change in the value of dichotomous variables and a one standard deviation change in the value of continuous variables while holding all other variables at their mean/modal values.

[b]A one standard deviation change in the Presidential Policy Signals measure is 3.16.

[c]A one standard deviation change in the Presidential Approval measure is 10.56

[d]A one standard deviation change in the Ideology measure is .68.

Table 9. Presidential Policy Influence Model: Logistic Regression Results for Justices' Voting on Labor Rights Policy Cases

Variable	M. L. E.	S. E.	Impact[a]
Presidential Policy Signaling	.7522	2.0700	—
Presidential Approval (base)	−.0056	.0057	—
Presidential Policy Signaling × Presidential Approval	.0514	.1677	
Justice Ideology	.4497**	.0705	7%[b]
Court Agenda	−.2050	.1611	—
Petitioner	.4393**	.0814	11%
Kennedy	.1418	.1643	—
Johnson	−.1477	.1790	—
Nixon	−.4365	.1810	—
Ford	−.0928	.2637	—
Carter	.0328	.2186	—
Reagan	−.1910	.1783	—
Bush	−.1329	.2163	—
Clinton	.0424	.3714	—
Constant	.2253	.1483	—

M. L. E. = maximum likelihood estimate; S. E. = standard error
Model chi square = 114.54, df = 14, P < .001
% correctly predicted = 59.50%
Null = 58.5%
Reduction in error = 2%
N = 2780

*Significant at .05

**Significant at .01

[a]The impact value displayed is the impact on the probability of a pro-labor rights vote for a one unit change in the value of dichotomous variables and a one standard deviation change in the value of continuous variables while holding all other variables at their mean/modal values.

[b]A one standard deviation change in the Ideology measure is .65.

Table 10. Presidential Policy Influence Model: Logistic Regression Results for Justices' Voting on Diplomacy Policy Cases

Variable	M. L. E.	S. E.	Impact[a]
Presidential Policy Signaling	−.0030	.0022	—
Presidential Approval (base)	−.0554**	.0133	—
Presidential Policy Signaling × Presidential Approval	.0030	.0022	—
Justice Ideology	1.0197**	.1411	−15%[b]
Court Agenda	−.2363	.2297	—
Petitioner	.1567	.1689	—
Kennedy	.2068	.2627	—
Johnson	1.3223	.4777	—
Nixon	1.9470	.3924	—
Ford	1.9777	.4782	—
Carter	1.2423	.4428	—
Reagan	.7385	.3306	—
Bush	−.6135	.5251	—
Clinton	.9248	1.7776	—
Constant	−.7395	.2302	—

M. L. E. = maximum likelihood estimate; S. E. = standard error
Model chi square = 114.01, df = 14, P < .001
% correctly predicted = 66.7%
Null = 50.7%
Reduction in error = 30%
N = 912

*Significant at .05

**Significant at .01

[a]The impact value displayed is the impact on the probability of a pro-liberal diplomacy vote for a one unit change in the value of dichotomous variables and a one standard deviation change in the value of continuous variables while holding all other variables at their mean/modal values.

[b]A one standard deviation change in the Ideology measure is .60.

Table 11. Presidential Policy Influence Model: Logistic Regression Results for Justices' Voting on Foreign Defense Policy Cases

Variable	M. L. E.	S. E.	Impact[a]
Presidential Policy Preferences	–.0202[†]	.0060	–9%[b]
Presidential Approval (base)	.0306**	.0121	—
Presidential Policy Preferences × Presidential Approval	.0007	.0006	
Justice Ideology	1.380**	.1360	18%[c]
Court Agenda	–.1522	.1892	—
Petitioner	.6485**	.1412	16%
Kennedy	.3600	.2828	—
Johnson	.7260	.2551	—
Nixon	.6160	.3602	—
Ford	2.7486	.6655	—
Carter	1.0091	.5412	—
Reagan	.0886	.3638	—
Bush	6.8674	5.2402	—
Clinton	1.2018	.4377	—
Constant	–1.1838	.2738	—

M. L. E. = maximum likelihood estimate; S. E. = standard error
Model chi square = 233.38, df = 14, P < .001
% correctly predicted = 68.70%
Null = 58.6%
Reduction in error = 23%
N = 1283

*Significant at .05

**Significant at .01

†Significant at .01 two-tailed test

[a]The Impact value displayed is the impact on the probability of a pro-liberal foreign defense vote for a one unit change in the value of dichotomous variables and a one standard deviation change in the value of continuous variables while holding all other variables at their mean/modal values.

[b]A one standard deviation change in the Presidential Policy Preferences measure is 18.11.

[c]A one standard deviation change in the Ideology measure is .55.

Table 12. Summary of Variables' Statistically Significant Effects on Justice Voting and Models' Overall Predictive Capabilities

Variable	Civil Rights	Law and Order	Labor Rights	Diplomacy Policy	Defense Policy
President Policy Preferences	Effect on Voting	Effect on Voting	No Effect on Voting	No Effect on Voting	Effect on Voting (Negative)
President Policy Preferences × President Approval	No Effect on Voting	Effect on Voting	No Effect on Voting	No Effect on Voting	No Effect on Voting
Justice Ideology	Effect on Voting	Effect on Voting	Effect on Voting	Effect on Voting	Effect on Voting
Court Agenda	No Effect on Voting	No Effect on Voting	No Effect on Voting	No Effect on Voting	No Effect on Voting
Petitioner	Effect on Voting	Effect on Voting	Effect on Voting	Effect on Voting	Effect on Voting
Model Reduction of Error	17.6%	31.3%	2%	30%	23%

susceptible to presidential rhetoric on criminal justice issues (see figure 14). This finding lends credence to Neustadt's (1990) assertion that the president's ability to persuade other political actors is intertwined with his public standing.[39] Presidential rhetorical signals have a statistically significant influence on justice policy-making in civil rights (albeit modest), and the effect does not appear to be conditioned by his public support. Indeed, presidents can evidently influence the Court to a certain degree,

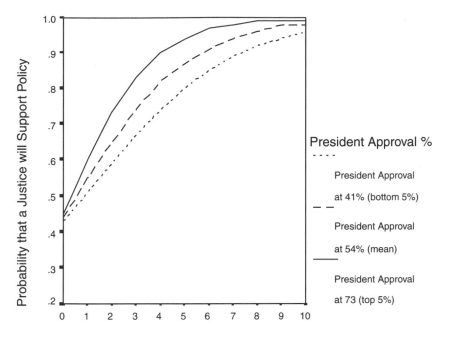

Presidential Rhetoric Supporting Policy (SUA %)

**Figure 14. The Interactive Effect of Presidential Rhetoric
and Presidential Approval on Justice Voting
in Law and Order Policy Cases**

through rhetoric on civil rights, whatever their public standing might be.

These findings provide evidence that is contrary to the predictions of prior studies (noted above) with regard to the effects of elite and public opinion on justice voting in different issue areas. Link (1995) suggests that the justices consider themselves to be leaders in civil rights policy and are not likely to be influenced by other government policy-makers. However, these results demonstrate that the president can affect justice voting on civil rights by going public on the issue. Flemming and Wood (1997) suggest that criminal procedure is not a salient issue and hence external influences do not affect justice voting behavior in this area. These findings demonstrate that not only are justices influenced by presidential rhetoric on law and order policy, but that they are further influenced by the amount of public backing presidents have when they go public on law and order.[40] Last, Wildavsky (1966) and others suggest that government actors afford the president more deference in foreign affairs than in domestic affairs. These results show that justices are unresponsive to presidential attempts to go public on diplomacy policy issues and, rather counterintuitively, are resistant to presidential policy rhetoric on foreign defense policy issues.

The Court Agenda variable results in all models suggest that the Court's legal agenda does not appear to play a significant role in justices' voting behavior in the issue areas examined. An alternative way of taking legal agenda effects into account is to focus on the legally relevant factual differences involved in a narrow subset of cases. In this situation, it is assumed that the legally relevant factual distinctions in cases are key to understanding how easy or difficult it will be for the justices to support a liberal or conservative position in a case (see Mishler and Sheehan 1996, 181). I performed such a model on a subset of law and order cases. The data analyzed are similar to that assessed by Segal and Spaeth (1993). It consists of search and seizure decisions by the Court from 1963 to 1990, in which the United States was a party (i.e., prosecutor).[41] I found that, consistent with the findings of Segal and Spaeth (1993), justices' votes were indeed influenced by legally relevant factual cues (e.g., location of the search, existence of a search warrant, etc.) as well as the justices' attitudinal preferences. However, I also found that justices were responsive to presidential rhetorical signaling concerning law and order in such search and seizure cases. Further, the ability of presidents to use such rhetoric to affect justice decision making in these cases is conditioned by their level of public approval.

It is also important to note that the Petitioner variable, which assesses the effect of litigant status on voting outcomes, yields statistically significant results. In all but one issue area (Diplomacy Policy), the policy in question is more likely to be supported by a justice when the party advancing the policy is appearing as a petitioner before the Court rather than as a respondent. While the executive case selection effects discussed in previous chapters are not relevant in this litigation situation, these results do support the general proposition that the Court takes on cases for review that it wishes to overturn. Hence, it is important to consider this factor in analyzing Supreme Court outcomes and justice voting.

Last, as demonstrated in table 12, the attitudinal model of judicial decision making is supported by these findings. The Justice Ideology variable exerts a statistically significant effect on justice voting in each of the issue areas examined.[42] However, what is not shown by the model's results is also telling. Given the strong assertions of advocates of the attitudinal model detailed previously, we might reasonably expect that no explanatory variable other than ideology would exert a statistically significant impact on justice voting. However, in only one issue area (Diplomacy Policy) is this found to be the case. Thus, while judicial attitudes are found to be a valuable explanation for judicial behavior, they are by no means conclusive. Other factors, including presidential rhetoric and presidential prestige, do exert a statistically significant influence on justice voting.

The President's Attorney: Can the Solicitor General Influence Supreme Court Policy-Making?

The solicitor general is responsible for a multitude of legal matters concerning the executive branch and handles almost all federal government litigation before the Supreme Court. The solicitor general's responsibilities involving Supreme Court litigation include, among others: (1) selecting cases that warrant petitions for certiorari to the Court when the federal government is a party; (2) submitting briefs opposing or supporting petitions for certiorari; (3) representing the federal government on the merits; (4) submitting amicus curiae briefs when the government is an interested party; and (5) authorizing other parties to intervene as amicus curiae when the government is a direct party (Salokar 1992, 12–13). In sum, the solicitor general is the primary legal advocate of the executive branch and the federal government before the Court, and it's representation involves all stages of Supreme Court litigation.

The solicitor general occupies a curious place in American institutional politics, in that he is an important player in both the judicial and executive branches. In fact, both branches rely heavily on the solicitor general's expertise and discretion. Scigliano (1971) notes that, "The solicitor general has succeeded in linking his services to both the executive and judicial branches and, as a consequence, in placing himself in the difficult, if challenging, position of trying to serve two masters" (162). With regard to the judicial branch, the Court relies on the solicitor general to act as a gatekeeper (by weeding out frivolous cases) and to provide informed and well-prepared briefs and oral argument (Salokar 1992). On the other hand, the president relies on the solicitor general as his primary legal arm in Supreme Court litigation, and the solicitor general is basically responsible for advancing the president's legal agenda in the Court (Deen, et al. 2000, Puro 1981, Salokar 1992, Segal 1988). Indeed, the president appoints the solicitor general (and can remove him), and the president and the solicitor general's office maintain frequent contacts about pending and potential matters before the Supreme Court (Deen et al. 2000, Puro 1981, Segal 1988). While solicitors general proclaim their independence from the executive office, Salokar seems to express the view of the majority of scholars that while the office enjoys functional, or organizational, autonomy from the president, "this independence does not translate into substantive freedom from the policies and politics of the White House" (1992, 175). Empirical studies tend to confirm the proposition that there is a general congruence between executive policy preferences and solicitor general positions before the Court (e.g., Meinhold and Shull 1998).

Solicitor general relations with the Court have been the topic of a good number of studies, most focusing on the spectacular degree of success that the office has had in litigating before the Court. Such studies have detailed the extraordinary success of the office in getting its cases heard by the Court (e.g., Caldeira and Wright 1988), its winning ways as a direct litigant before the Court (e.g., Salokar 1992), and its ability to influence Court outcomes through amicus participation (e.g., Segal 1988, Segal and Reedy 1988). It is perhaps this overwhelmingly successful record before the Court that has led many scholars to conclude that the solicitor general enjoys a special relationship and advantage with the Court.

The solicitor general's rather unique dual role as executive advocate and Court confidant was well-summarized by Ronald

Reagan's Solicitor General, Rex Lee, who in a 1985 interview explained:

> On the one hand, I am a presidential appointee, a part of the president's team. I very much believe in the president's program and I want to do what I can to help advance it. And there are ways that I can help it by helping to shape and to guide the development of Supreme Court law. On the other hand, I am also an officer of the court. And the relationship between the solicitor general and the Supreme Court is one that knows no counterpart. (Witt 1986,120)

The general consensus of practitioners and scholars is that, in addition to sometimes being referred to as the "Tenth Justice" (Caplan 1987, 3) and maintaining an office in the Supreme Court building (Salokar 1992, 2), the solicitor general's office enjoys a unique advantage with the Court and carries special influence when it appears as a litigant (e.g., Caplan 1987, Salokar 1992, Segal and Spaeth 1993).

In 1998 Kevin McGuire put a bit of a hole in the generally accepted view that the solicitor general has a special relationship with the Court, which translates into the office having a unique litigation advantage. He maintains that there is a lack of empirical evidence to support the various rationales for solicitor general success with the Court, which include: the Court rewards the office's careful selection of cases, the Court rewards the (alleged) neutrality and independence of the office, and the Court defers to the prestige of the office and the executive branch generally (1998, 507–10). While McGuire concedes that the solicitor general's presence before the Court is a powerful predictor of Court outcomes (i.e., the Court will inordinately decide in the solicitor general's favor), he astutely points out that the argument that the solicitor general enjoys a special advantage with the Court because the office wins—and that the office wins due to special advantage—is essentially circular reasoning (508). In other words, scholars maintain that the solicitor general's office enjoys a unique advantage and point to the explanatory power of the litigation status of the solicitor general's office (its presence or absence) to prove this special advantage. However, McGuire notes that the solicitor general is a classical "repeat player" and suggests that if controls are introduced to account for litigant experience before the Court, then the office should be no more successful than a number of other Supreme Court repeat-player litigants (520–22).

He compiles an impressive data set of Supreme Court cases (from 1977–82), which allows him to assess the litigation advantage (successfulness) of parties while controlling for the relative Supreme Court litigation experience of the attorneys involved. He finds that the solicitor general does not fare significantly better before the Court than other litigants when such controls are introduced, and concludes that there is no empirical foundation for the commonly held belief that the solicitor general has any unique relationship with, or advantage before, the Court (520–22).

Thus, the generally accepted view that the executive (via the solicitor general) enjoys a special litigation advantage in the Supreme Court appears, to some degree, to hinge upon the manner in which it has traditionally been modeled. Most studies on the office use a simple dichotomous variable indicating the solicitor general's presence as a litigant and the corresponding coefficient indicating that the office is uncommonly successful relative to other parties. Of course, even McGuire admits that there are considerable practical difficulties in directly accounting for all Supreme Court litigants' relative experience, and that this factor has no doubt restricted the ability of many studies to control for such influences.

However, is it perhaps possible to assess the influence of the solicitor general in another manner? Given the findings detailed previously in this chapter—indicating that, in some circumstances, the president can influence Court policy indirectly by sending public-rhetoric signals concerning legal policy—is it possible that the solicitor general can also send important executive policy signals through its litigation actions?

I assess this proposition by employing a model substantially similar to the one used to examine the effect of presidential rhetorical signaling on justices' policy making. In order to discern executive policy signals emanating from the solicitor general's office, I turn to the office's use of amicus curiae briefs. Since the solicitor general's office can take either side of a given Supreme Court dispute as an amicus participant, it is in this litigation role that the

executive branch, through the solicitor general's office, has perhaps the most discretion in attempting to shape Supreme Court
policy (Segal and Reedy 1987, Segal 1988, Deen, et al. 2000).

To make operational solicitor generals' policy signals I consider the ideological direction of the solicitor generals' amicus
briefs in civil liberties cases. Fortunately, data on solicitor general
amicus filings have been collected for previous studies and I use
this available data to create an annual measure of solicitor general civil liberties policy signals from 1955 to 1981.[43] I then use
this measure to analyze the effect of such policy signaling on
justices' voting in all law and order cases and civil rights cases
generally. The solicitor general policy-signal measure is then
interacted with presidential public approval to discern whether
any effect of executive policy signaling, through amicus activity
on justices' decision making, is conditioned on the public prestige of the executive.[44]

Table 13 details the results of this model for both Law and
Order cases and Civil Rights cases. Note that in order to provide
intuitive hypotheses and results, the directionality of executive
amicus activity is adjusted so that the percentage of conservative
amicus briefs filed are used for Law and Order cases, whereas the
inverse (the percentage of liberal amicus briefs filed) are used
for Civil Rights cases. The models' chi-square statistics indicate
that the models are sufficient for explanation in both sets of
cases and both have respectable predictive capabilities (Law and
Order provides a 34% reduction of predictive error, and 22% for
Civil Rights). In both models the effect of executive policy signaling through amicus activity is statistically significant. However,
the effect of such signaling is only conditional on the president's
public standing in the context of Law and Order cases. As the
Law and Order interactive results show, while the coefficient of
the component term, S. G. Conservative Briefs %, is negative,
the coefficient of the interactive term, S. G. Briefs %—Presidential Approval, is positive. Hence, the overall effect of solicitor
general signals is positive, but contingent upon presidential prestige (see figure 15). Substantively, the probability impact of amicus signaling in the Civil Rights model is fairly modest, with a
one standard deviation change in signaling yielding only about
a 3% change in the probability of a pro-civil rights vote. A change
over the range of the variable (30% to 100%) yields an impact

Table 13. Solicitor General Amicus Policy Signals Influence Model, 1955–81: Logistic Regression Results for Justices' Voting

Law and Order Policy Cases		Civil Rights Policy Cases	
Variable	M. L. E.	Variable	M. L. E.
S. G. Conservative Briefs %	−.0134** (.0024)	S. G. Liberal Briefs %	.0106** (.0030)
Presidential Approval	.0028 (.0034)	Presidential Approval	−.0084* (.0037)
S. G. Briefs % × Presidential Approval	.0005** (.0002)	S. G. Briefs % × Presidential Approval	.0003 (.0002)
President Policy Signals (Rhetoric)	.0230* (.0111)	President Policy Signals (Rhetoric)	.0336* (.0160)
Justice Ideology	−1.2574** (.0503)	Justice Ideology	.9959** (.0468)
Court Agenda	−.0934 (.1203)	Court Agenda	−.1561 (.1556)
Petitioner	.8105** (.0638)	Petitioner	.8274** (.0610)
Kennedy	−.3683 (.1291)	Kennedy	.9023 (.1612)
Johnson	.0817 (.1405)	Johnson	.1139 (.1625)
Nixon	.0997 (.1468)	Nixon	.6321 (.1624)
Ford	−.0238 (.1448)	Ford	.3788 (.1557)
Carter	−.4519 (.1200)	Carter	.2167 (.1458)
Reagan	.2404 (.2078)	Reagan	.8858 (.1863)
Constant	−.2954** (.0864)	Constant	−.5367** (.1240)

M.L.E. = maximum likelihood estimate
Model chi square = 1102, P < .000
% correctly predicted = 67.28%
Null = 52.42%
Reduction in error = 34%
N = 6446
*Significant at .05
**Significant at .01

M.L.E. = maximum likelihood estimate
Model chi square = 951, P < .000
% correctly predicted = 68.76%
Null = 59.88%
Reduction in error = 22%
N = 6072
*Significant at .05
**Significant at .01

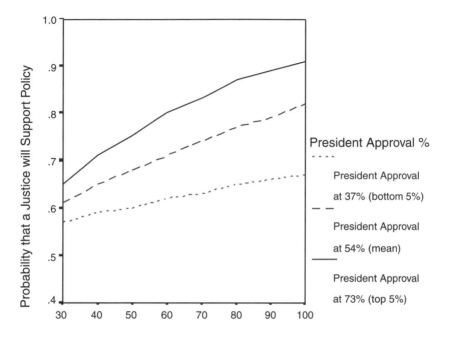

Figure 15. The Interactive Effect of Solicitor General Amicus Signals and Presidential Approval on Justice Voting in Law and Order Policy Cases

of approximately 13%. As demonstrated in figure 15, and in contrast to the Civil Rights model, the probability impact of amicus signaling in the Law and Order context ranges from modest, when presidential public standing is low, to fairly pronounced when the president enjoys relatively high levels of public prestige.

These results indicate that, much like presidential policy rhetoric, the amicus activities of the executive branch can work as policy signals and affect the decision making of the justices in cases generally, rather than just those in which the solicitor general appears as a litigant. Of course, these findings are not aimed toward directly addressing the findings and conclusions of McGuire concerning the leveling effect of experience on the assumed unique litigation advantage of the solicitor general's office. Rather, this analysis suggests that there may be ways, beyond simply by winning individual cases before the Court, that the solicitor general and the executive branch may influence

Supreme Court policy. Thus, this examination of the solicitor general's signaling activities provides another beneficial piece of information toward comprehending the complicated relationship between the executive and the Court.

Discussion

If indeed, the power of the presidency is the power to persuade, then the power of the president to influence the policy-making of the judicial branch of the federal government should be of interest to presidency, judicial, and policy scholars alike. This chapter's findings provide intriguing insight as to the bounds of presidential influence on the decision making of the Supreme Court justices in policy areas in which presidents have traditionally expressed preferences (either through policy rhetoric or amicus activity). Further, this study reveals that in at least one major policy area (i.e., Law and Order cases), presidential prestige is a source of capital that presidents can bring to bear in influencing the policy-making of the Supreme Court.

While the power of the president to influence the policy-making of the federal judiciary through appointment has been a popular source of study (e.g., Stidham and Carp 1987, Abraham 1992) this examination of president-Court relations demonstrates presidential influence on Supreme Court justice policy-making beyond mere appointment. Certainly presidents can affect Court policy-making by appointing like-minded justices, however, this particular path toward influencing Court policy is limited to the degree that the appointment opportunity arises during a president's administration. This study demonstrates that presidents can use their tools of rhetoric, amicus activity, and popular prestige toward this same end. In short, presidents can contemporaneously affect the voting decisions of Supreme Court justices by sending public signals of their policy preferences.

The results of chapters 3 and 4 demonstrate that the president's litigation success before the Court (either directly concerning his formal powers of office or via his bureaucratic agents) may be benefitted by his popularity and support from the public. In this chapter we see that the president can use signaling tools and public prestige to affect the policy direction of the Court more generally, at least in certain policy areas. Thus, the general thesis of this book—that the president can use public prestige as political capital in interactions with the Court—receives some support in all three president-Court engagements examined. While the analyses presented do provide support for more traditional explanations of justice decision making (e.g., attitudes), this study also advances our understanding of president-Court relations by showing that considerations such as presidential signaling and presidential public prestige can be influential factors in Supreme Court justice decision making in situations in which the president has a general vested interest in Court policy outcomes.

Chapter Six

Conclusion

T his study imparts useful information concerning the political power of the presidency when interacting with another branch of government and also provides insight as to the general decision-making process of the Supreme Court justices. To conclude, I review the generalizable findings presented above and discuss how they augment our understanding of these two primary national political institutions. First, I focus on how this study contributes to our knowledge of the Supreme Court and justice voting behavior. Second, I discuss the potential ramifications of this study for presidential strategy with regard to relations with the Supreme Court.

The Supreme Court

Studies on the Supreme Court have been traditionally dominated by examination of the impact of justices' backgrounds and attitudes on their voting behavior. However, recent studies have considered the impact of a wide range of influences on the behavior of judicial actors, including institutional factors (e.g., Brace and Hall 1993), external forces (Mishler and Sheehan 1993, 1996, Flemming and Wood 1997), and consideration for the reactions of the other branches of government (Segal 1997). In this study I find that a number of attitudinal, political, and external factors affect Supreme Court justice voting in cases involving interactions with the executive.

First, the above analyses indicate that the ideologies of the justices do influence their voting behavior. This is found to be the case in all three of the president-Court interactions examined. In chapter 3, the prevalent theory from the presidency literature concerning liberals' views toward presidential power is corroborated: liberal justices are indeed skeptical of presidential power and tend to vote against the president in presidential power cases. Chapter 4 reveals that justices tend to be deferential toward agency actions that are in accord with their own ideological preferences. In chapter 5 justice ideology is found to be a statistically significant determinant of justice voting in each of the policy areas examined. Thus, the findings presented here do much to corroborate the assertion of Segal and Spaeth (1993) that attitudes matter. However, what we do not find in these models is that the attitudes of the justices dictate or determine their voting decisions. Factors other than justice attitudes are found to influence justices' voting as well. Therefore, perhaps an integrated model better describes the justices' decision calculus in presidency-Court interactions. As Baum (1999) notes, the behavior of Supreme Court justices largely reflects the interplay between their traits as individuals and the situations in which they make decisions (213).

Second, political considerations matter in justices' treatment of the executive in Supreme Court litigation. Some support is provided for the proposition that justices loyally support their appointing presidents and their bureaucratic agents. While justices are appointed for life tenure and ostensibly have no higher judicial ambitions, these findings indicate that some degree of allegiance is conferred to the political actor responsible for their elevation to the Court. However, the lack of a statistically significant finding with regard to the same party variable indicates that this allegiance does not extend to a justice's political party. Additionally, some support is provided for the two presidencies thesis, which dictates that political actors are more apt to defer to the executive in matters of foreign policy than on domestic policy matters. However, while this proposition holds true as to presidential power cases and with foreign policy agencies, the analyses concerning presidential policy preferences indicate that justices are resistant to executive rhetoric in their decisions on foreign defense policy issues.

Third, this study provides intriguing information concerning the democratic nature of the Supreme Court. While the democratic nature of the Court has been a perennial source of academic debate in the field of judicial politics, it has become especially prominent in recent years (see Flemming and Wood 1997, Mishler and Sheehan 1993, 1996, Norpoth and Segal 1994). In these analyses I find that one of the most well-known measures of public opinion (presidential approval) can affect the behavior of perhaps the most elite and independent officials of the federal government, the Supreme Court justices. In this sense, they do not act too differently from other political actors (e.g., members of Congress). The results presented here demonstrate that justices reference presidential approval in their direct interactions with the executive (presidential power cases), their treatment of the president's bureaucratic agencies and, to some degree, in their substantive policy voting decisions. Furthermore, I find that justices are also influenced by another external source, presidential policy signals in the fields of civil rights and law and order. In sum, these findings lend support to the notion that Supreme Court justices do not act strictly on sincere policy preferences in their voting decisions; they are swayed by external majoritarian and elite concerns. While my findings here will by no means settle the longstanding debate on the democratic nature of the Supreme Court, they will hopefully add beneficial new perspectives to this important academic discussion.

The Presidency

Lyn Ragsdale (1998) argues that presidents could learn a great deal about the presidency from political scientists. She notes, "Few presidents seem ever to have taken a course on the presidency; some seem to have failed one. Presidents typically presume that by virtue of being in office they must know the job's ins and outs. Yet, political scientists understand the presidency in a way that other experts cannot. Presidents could benefit from studying the presidency" (1998, 29). She adds that political science research has yielded generalizations about the presidency that could be heeded by the president to avoid the potential pitfalls of the office. I submit that presidents could learn something valuable about their office, and their interactions with the Supreme Court, from the results presented in this book.

Essentially, the findings presented here suggest general strategies that are likely to improve the president's fortune before the Court.

First, the power of appointment is certainly a useful tool to the extent that it is available to the president. Through the power of appointment presidents can change the ideological composition of the Court. Furthermore, presidents receive deference from their appointees even when holding the ideological preferences of the justices constant. In other words, presidents' appointees show a degree of allegiance or loyalty to the presidents who put them on the Court beyond a mere ideological correlation between them and their appointing presidents.

Second, the president can improve his lot before the Court by being strategic in the cases that he and his bureaucratic agents appeal to the Court. The litigation status (petitioner or respondent) of the executive has differential effects on outcomes depending upon the degree of case selection discretion that the Supreme Court enjoys. In high-profile cases concerning the formal powers of the executive office the Court's case selection discretion is politically constrained (Perry 1991) and consequently, the Court is apt to affirm the decisions of its lower court brethren. Hence, the president should prudently consider the merits and precedent value of cases before petitioning the Court to take on lower court losses in such presidential power cases. Alternatively, the Court enjoys wide discretion in the selection of agency cases that it reviews. In these cases, the presidents' bureaucracies tend to be favored more when they appear before the Court as petitioners rather than as respondents. It is possible that this is due to careful case selection strategy by the executive branch. Presidents would be wise to consider using a similar strategy in the formal presidential power cases mentioned above. Presidents might also be well-advised to consider the political sphere in which they are operating in their case selection decisions. The fabled two presidencies thesis receives some support from the analyses presented here. Generally, Supreme Court justices are more receptive to the president and his bureaucratic agencies when the case involves foreign policy considerations, rather than domestic concerns.

Last, presidents can use their tools of persuasion and prestige to gain support in the Supreme Court. The power of presidential policy signaling is evinced in the results of this study. In the areas of civil rights and law and order, presidents are able to influence justices' policy voting by going public with signals of their policy preferences, either through the amicus activity of the president's legal arm or through public rhetoric.

Furthermore, presidents can improve their prospects before the Court by cultivating their public prestige. The notion that presidential prestige is a source of political capital that presidents can draw upon to influence other political actors has been examined extensively with regard to president-Congress relations. However, with rare exception, scholars have not been inclined to argue that presidential prestige can help make presidents more successful with the judicial branch. In this study I test a celebrated theory of president-Congress relations on the relationship between the president and the Supreme Court justices. I find that indeed, in certain circumstances, presidents can use public approval as a source of political capital in relations with the Supreme Court justices.

Future Research

The aim of this study has been to add to our knowledge of presidency-Court relations by providing generalizable empirical findings on hypotheses concerning the determinants of presidential success with the Court. I find that general extra-legal theories, suggested by the relevant presidential and judicial politics literature, help to explain presidential success before the Court in three distinct litigation circumstances in which the president and the Court interface.

For the most part, interactions between the president and the Court have been traditionally examined in a narrative manner that focuses on specific case analysis and anecdotal accounts. While this approach provides rich descriptive detail and valuable historical information, it fails to furnish generalizable explanations of presidency-Court relations. King (1993) laments that "alhough probably more has been written about the presidency than all other areas of American politics combined, most work in the field is not yet to the point where concepts are to be measured and theories tested systematically" (387). Future work on president-Court relations, qualitative or quantitative, should strive to provide such systematic theories.

Notes

Chapter Two

1. While the Supreme Court ordinarily enjoys extraordinary discretion in its selection of cases to review, I examine a particular litigation situation in chapter 3 (presidential power cases) in which the Court's discretion in this regard is politically constrained.

2. The two presidencies thesis is directly tested as a hypothesis in chapters 3 and 4. However, in chapter 5 the research design utilized is not conducive to this approach. In chapter 5, I examine generally the Court justices' decision making in the area of foreign policy and I test hypotheses on the effect of presidential rhetoric and presidential approval on justice voting in this issue area.

Chapter Three

3. See also Ducat and Dudley (1989b).

4. I associate specific Court decisions to particular presidents by the exact dates of presidential tenure. In other words, the president who is in office when a case is heard by the Court is associated with that case. This is consistent with Ducat and Dudley (1989a). I do not make the exception that some cases were "personal" to Richard Nixon and assign them to him regardless of who the president was when the case was heard by the Court. Ducat and Dudley follow this rule and also assign Nixon's presidential approval scores at the end of his term to the case for the Presidential Prestige variable.

5. Despite the fact that presidents' vote record was lower than their case record in Ducat and Dudley's district court study, the presidents won 61% of the actual presidential-power court cases. This indicates that they won the close cases and lost by large vote margins.

6. Ducat and Dudley (1989a) included a dummy variable to control for the idiosyncracies of the Nixon administration. They reasoned

that the Nixon cases dominated their sample, both in terms of total cases and presidential losses. I choose to incorporate administration variables for all presidents in order to control for any administration effects that may occur.

7. Generally, where appellate courts' discretion is constrained (e.g., state supreme courts which do not have intermediate appellate courts) the judicial norm is actually to affirm the lower court, and hence favor respondents (Baum 1994).

8. It is also tenable that when the president has lost at the lower court level, his case is not as meritorious as when he has won in the lower court and is appearing as a respondent.

9. As demonstrated in figure 2, the selection process can be quite complicated and involves several actors whose decisions might affect whether the president appears as a petitioner or respondent. Indeed, the likelihood that the president appears as a petitioner or as a respondent may be partially attributable to the strategic decisions of his litigation opponents. However, it is likely that much of the same phenomena that are apt to encourage the president to bring his case to the Supreme Court correspond to the factors that would discourage litigation opponents from hauling the president into the Supreme Court.

10. The technique incorporated here is a modified, yet consistent, version of the procedure suggested by Heckman (1979). Heckman used the inverse of Mill's ratio (a monotone decreasing function of the probability that an observation is selected into the sample of interest) to assess selection effects. Alternatively, I use predicted probability estimates to assess such selection effects.

11. Here, I use a lagged (one year) version of the presidential approval variable. The lagged measure was used, since the president's decision to bring a case to the Court is made well before the case is heard by the Court. This measure should more accurately reflect the political climate in which the president makes the decision to appeal his case.

12. Appointment was found to be a significant determinant of presidential support—at the .05 level in the Basic Model and at the .10 level in the revised model.

Chapter Four

13. Justice Rehnquist's opinion (concurring in part and dissenting in part from the majority opinion of Justice White) was joined by Justices Burger, Powell, and O'Connor.

14. This efficient design is especially helpful, given that interactive terms are employed in my analysis of agencies before the Court.

15. For instance, in a judicial power case the Court may decide in favor of "access" to the court system, while the party seeking access may be seeking a substantively conservative outcome.

16. These include all formally decided cases that had oral arguments.

17. Zorn's (1997a) examination of the federal government before the Court notes that the government's success in gaining access to the Court has been stable over time, while other litigants have experienced decreasing success in getting their cases heard by the Court. Thus, federal government access to the Court appears to have increased over time relative to other litigants. Agency trial court litigation trends are difficult to track due to the lack of readily obtainable data. The Administrative Office of the United States Courts has been keeping statistical information on agency district court litigation since 1990. Agency cases in the U.S. District Courts have increased from 2,558 in 1990 to 4,412 in 1997 (personal communication with the Administrative Office of the U.S. Courts–Statistical Division).

18. Cases are associated with the level of presidential approval of the president in office when the cases are decided by the Supreme Court. The assumption that presidents prefer for their agencies to receive deferential review (i.e., be successful) before the Court is supported by the fact that the president (through the Department of Justice and the solicitor general's office) has great discretion over the appellate litigation direction of the federal agencies (Devins 1994). Thus, in the hypothetical instance in which a president does not agree with an agency's specific litigation stance (perhaps due to a litigation policy advanced by a prior administration) he could simply decline to pursue the case at the Supreme Court level.

19. To prevent overlap between categories, the Department of State and the Department of Veterans' Affairs are considered to be "cabinet agencies," thus this variable represents non-cabinet level agencies that deal with foreign/military affairs policy.

20. The criteria for determining the liberal/conservative direction of an agency decision is consistent with Sheehan (1990, 1992) and derives from the coding of cases found in the U.S. Supreme Court Judicial Database (ICPSR 9422, Harold Spaeth principle investigator). Essentially, decisions favoring unions, consumers, environmental protection, economic underdogs, civil liberty claimants, etc. are coded liberal and decisions against these interests are coded conservative.

21. Sheehan (1992) assessed the proximity issue by comparing independent regulatory agencies with agencies that he deemed to be "executive" in nature. Sheehan notes that his categorization scheme of the federal agencies is by no means dispositive and that any categorization

attempt is, to some degree, arbitrary. I believe that the cabinet agencies represent best those agencies that are closely tied to White House politics and presidential partisan concerns. Hence, I choose this categorization scheme to assess the proximity issue.

22. For instance, a 40% change in presidential approval (at the top end of the variable range of 35% to 76%) would yield approximately a 17% change in the probability that a justice would vote for an agency, holding the other variables at their mean/modal values.

23. I also tested an "overall" public approval measure which was essentially the trend of the president's level of approval from his first year in office to the year of the case. The variable did not approach statistical significance.

24. I also tested the effect of justices' party affiliation on voting. The measurement was coded 1 for Democrat, 0 for independent (i.e., Frankfurter), and −1 for Republican, thus the scale is the same as the justice ideology measure. The maximum likelihood coefficient was statistically significant at conventional levels, but was weaker in impact than the justice ideology coefficient.

25. Zorn (2001, 1997a, 1997b) explains that the decision to appeal agency cases to the Supreme Court is a joint function of the Department of Justice's office and the solicitor general's office. The Department of Justice's office screens cases and makes recommendations concerning case selection that the solicitor general's office can either accept or reject. Typically, the solicitor general's office accepts most recommendations made by the Department of Justice.

26. This hypothesis was assessed with an interaction term (along with base terms) similar to that used in the basic model. The interaction term and base coefficients indicate that agencies making liberal decisions are more likely to appear as petitioners when the Court's cumulative ideological composition is more liberal. Further, agencies making conservative decisions are less likely to appear as petitioners when the Court's ideology is more liberal.

27. Drawing upon Zorn (1997a, 1997b) and others, I hypothesized that the executive branch would be more likely to appeal lower court losses in cases dealing with economic matters (the reference category) than cases dealing with criminal procedure, civil liberties, and labor issues. The coefficients for the latter three categories indicate that indeed, agencies were less likely to appear as petitioners when the cases involved these issues than when the case involved economic matters. I also hypothesized that the executive branch would be more concerned with losses in constitutional cases (as opposed to statutory cases) and therefore would be more likely to appeal lower court losses when constitutional issues were involved. The coefficient for the constitutional

issue variable indicates that the executive branch is more likely to appear as a petitioner when the case turns on constitutional issues.

28. I again used a lagged (one year) version of the presidential approval variable. The lagged measure was used since the decision by the executive branch (Department of Justice and solicitor general) is typically made well before the actual substantive decision on the case by the Court.

29. As in chapter 3, in using the Heckman (1979) procedure I create a variable from the predicted probabilities estimates of the selection effects model regression. Then, I run a model substantially similar to the basic model (on justice votes for agencies) on only the strategically brought cases (i.e., the cases in which the agency appears as a petitioner). In this model I include the Predicted Probabilities variable to test whether the strategic effects assessed in the selection model affect the likelihood that a justice will vote for an agency.

Chapter Five

30. This number is then multiplied by one hundred to provide a more intuitive measure that reflects the percentage of the president's State of the Union message that was devoted to promoting that particular policy.

31. Intercoder reliability scores for presidential rhetoric on the four issue areas were as follows: Civil Rights–95%, Law and Order–95%, Labor Rights–97%, and Foreign Policy–92%. In a few years, presidents beginning a new administration did not give a formal State of the Union message. For those years speeches that most closely approximated the State of the Union message were used as surrogates for the formal message. These include: Nixon–1969 (Inaugural Address), Nixon–1973 (State of the Union Overview and Goals Address), Carter–1977 (Report to the American People), Reagan–1981 (Inaugural Address), Bush–1989 (Address on Administration Goals), and Clinton–1993 (Address on Administration Goals).

32. The time period examined is 1953 to 1995, thus, part of the Eisenhower administration is not encompassed as well as the later years of the Clinton administration.

33. Mishler and Sheehan (1996) note that as the Court's ideological balance (and hence, agenda) becomes more conservative, it becomes harder for an individual justice (whose ideology has remained consistent over time) to support conservative positions, and vice versa. While Mishler and Sheehan use an aggregate Court ideological score (based on Segal, et al.'s 1995 measures of justices' summed ideologies for a given year), I found in preliminary analyses of the data that this

method yielded some multicollinearity concerns so I instead use an alternative method of tapping the Court's ideological balance—democratic majority control—as noted in the text.

34. The litigation situation studied in this chapter is the typical situation in which the Court has enormous discretion in choosing the cases that it wants to hear. This is counter to the situation, found in chapter 3, in which the Court's discretion in choosing cases for review is politically constrained.

35. In the civil rights and law and order data sets, Reagan's administration was the most prevalent, whereas in the labor rights, diplomacy, and foreign policy data sets Eisenhower's administration was the most prevalent.

36. Both Link (1995) and Flemming and Wood (1997) draw their conclusions regarding which issue areas fit into their categories (Court leadership areas and high saliency areas, respectively) only after assessing their findings. Therefore, their categorization of certain issue areas is formulated in a rather ad-hoc manner. Link (1995) suggests that the Court may consider itself a leader in civil rights policy (and resist external influences), as opposed to criminal procedure cases where it may be more susceptible to elite preferences (e.g., the president and Congress). In contrast, Fleming and Wood (1997) argue that civil rights cases, along with civil liberties, judicial power, and taxation cases, are more salient than criminal procedure, economic, and labor cases. They argue that these high-saliency cases should be more susceptible to external influences in justice voting. Thus, the literature on this issue is not entirely consistent and no cohesive theory emerges to discern which issue areas (civil rights, labor rights, law and order) are particularly resistant or susceptible to external influences.

37. A finding that presidential policy rhetoric influences justices' decision making on civil rights issues certainly undermines Link's (1995) assertion that the justices perceive themselves as leaders in this area and are therefore not influenced by the preferences of other elite political actors. Further, a similar finding with regard to law and order policy calls into question Fleming and Wood's (1997) assertion that justices are resistant to external influences on criminal procedure issues (due to lack of saliency).

38. Note that, due to the accompanying interaction term, the effect of presidential policy signals reflected in these tables is conditional. Thus, the manner of the effect may vary according to the level of the other interaction term, here presidential approval (see Freidrich 1982). The conditional effects of presidential policy signals in all issue areas are assessed at the mean level of presidential approval.

39. I also tested an "overall" public approval measure, which was essentially the trend of the president's level of approval from his first year in office to the year of the case. The variable was in the predicted direction and statistically significant at the .10 level for diplomacy policy cases and at the .01 level in law and order cases. The variable did not attain statistical significance in any other policy areas.

40. It might also be argued that justices are more protective of their constitutional law decisions, and should be more receptive to presidential influences on statutory decisions, where they may be later overridden by a president/Congress initiative (e.g., Segal 1997). In order to assess this possibility, I examined separately the sub-categories of cases in which the Court reviewed the constitutionality of government decisions and those in which constitutional review was not involved, in each of the issue areas studied. No systematic differences between the two sub-categories emerged with regard to the influence of external factors.

41. I am indebted to Jeffrey Segal, who generously supplied the data for this auxiliary analysis. Of course, he bears no responsibility for the analysis or interpretations presented here.

42. I also tested the effect of justices' party affiliations on voting. The measurement was coded 1 for Democrat, 0 for independent (i.e., Frankfurter), and −1 for Republican. Thus, the scale is the same as the justice ideology measure. In all issue areas the maximum likelihood coefficient was statistically significant at conventional levels, but was weaker in impact than the justice ideology coefficient.

43. This general data on solicitor general amicus briefs was generously provided to me by Jeffrey Segal and has been analyzed in previous publications (Segal and Reedy 1987, Segal 1988). However, he bears no responsibility for the analysis or interpretations presented here. Civil liberties cases include cases concerning criminal procedure, civil rights, First Amendment, due process, privacy, and attorney issues, as categorized by the Spaeth U.S. Supreme Court Judicial Database (see e.g., Epstein, Segal, Spaeth, and Walker 1996). As noted in the text, I use this measure to test the effect of solicitor general signaling on justices' voting in Law and Order and Civil Rights cases. Since cases involving solicitor general amicus filings on issues of foreign policy and labor policy were extremely rare, I restrict my analysis to Law and Order and Civil Rights cases. Combining amicus case filings into the civil liberties category had the side benefit of increasing the number of cases per year to a suitable amount in order to provide a reasonably stable measure of the ideological direction of solicitor general briefs. Still, some years had few total civil liberties cases. In the five years in

which there were fewer than four civil liberties cases with solicitor general amicus briefs filed, I substituted the value derived from analysis of the ideological direction of all solicitor general amicus briefs filed for that year. The solicitor general civil liberties briefs variable is basically the percentage of briefs either conservative or liberal (% conservative for the Law and Order model and % liberal for the Civil Rights model) during a calendar year. It is matched with the Court's term and this method provides a natural lag of approximately nine months in this variable.

44. In this model I also control for presidential rhetorical signaling, and in fact it is found to be significant in both the Civil Rights and Law and Order contexts. However, in order to facilitate straightforward interpretation of the S.G. Briefs %—Presidential Approval interaction (and prevent potential multicollinearity concerns) I do not include an interaction for presidential rhetorical signals—presidential approval.

References

Abraham, Henry, J. 1992. *Justices and Presidents*. New York: Oxford University Press.

Adamany, David W. and Joel B. Grossman. 1983. "Support for the Supreme Court as a National Policymaker." *Law and Policy Quarterly* 5:405–37.

Aldrich, John H. and Forrest D. Nelson. 1984. *Linear Probability, Logit and Probit Models*. Beverly Hills: Sage.

Baum, Lawrence. 1988. "Measuring Policy Change in the U.S. Supreme Court." *The American Political Science Review* 82: 905–12.

Baum, Lawrence. 1992. "Membership Change and Collective Voting Change in the United States Supreme Court." *Journal of Politics* 54(1):3–24.

Baum, Lawrence. 1994. *American Courts: Process and Policy, 3rd Edition*. Boston: Houghton-Mifflin.

Baum, Lawrence. 1999. "Recruitment and Motivations of Supreme Court Justices." In *Supreme Court Decision Making: New Institutionalist Approaches*, eds. Cornell Clayton and Howard Gillman. Chicago: University of Chicago Press.

Biskupic, Joan and Elder Witt. 1997. *Congressional Quarterly's Guide to the U.S. Supreme Court, Third Edition*. Washington, D.C.: Congressional Quarterly, Inc.

Bond, Jon R. and Richard Fleisher. 1990. *The President in the Legislative Arena*. Chicago: University of Chicago Press.

Brace, Paul and Melinda Gann Hall. 1990. "Neo-institutionalism and Dissent in State Supreme Courts." *Journal of Politics* 52:54–70.

Brace, Paul and Barbara Hinckley. 1992. *Follow the Leader: Opinion Polls and the Modern Presidents.* New York: Basic Books.

Brace, Paul and Melinda Gann Hall. 1993. "Integrated Models of Judicial Dissent." *Journal of Politics* 55:914–45.

Brenner, Saul, Timothy M. Hagle, and Harold J. Spaeth. 1990. "Increasing the Size of Minimum Winning Original Coalitions on the Warren Court." *Polity* 23:309–18.

Brody, Richard A. 1991. *Assessing the President: The Media, Elite Opinion, and Public Support.* Stanford, CA: Stanford University Press.

Caldeira, Gregory A. 1986. "Neither Purse or the Sword: The Dynamics of Public Confidence in the United States Supreme Court." *American Political Science Review* 80:1209–26.

Caldeira, Gregory A. 1987. "Public Opinion and the U.S. Supreme Court: FDR's Court-Packing Plan." *American Political Science Review* 81:1139–53.

Caldeira, Gregory A. 1991. "Courts and Public Opinion." In *The American Courts: A Critical Assessment,* ed. John B. Gates and Charles A. Johnson. Washington, D.C.: Congressional Quarterly Press.

Cableira, Gregory A. and John Wright. 1988. "Organized Interests and Agenda Setting in the U.S. Supreme Court." *American Political Science Review* 82:1109–27.

Caldeira, Gregory A. and James Gibson. 1992. "The Etiology of Public Support for the Supreme Court." *American Journal of Political Science* 36:635–64.

Campbell, James E. and Joe A. Sumners. 1990. "Presidential Coattails in Senate Elections." *American Political Science Review* 84: 513–524.

Canon, Bradley C. and Michael Giles. 1972. "Recurring Litigants: Federal Agencies Before the Supreme Court." *Western Political Quarterly* 25: 183–91.

Caplan, Lincoln. 1987. *The Tenth Justice: The Solicitor General and the Rule of Law.* New York: Alfred A. Knopf.

Casper, Jonathan D. 1976. "The Supreme Court and National Policy-Making." *American Political Science Review* 70:50–66.

Cohen, Jeffrey E. 1993. "The Dynamics and Interaction between the President's and the Public's Civil Rights Agendas: A Study in Presidential Leadership and Representation." *Policy Studies Journal* 21:514–21.

Cohen, Jeffrey. 1995. "Presidential Rhetoric and the Public Agenda." *American Journal of Political Science* 39:87–107.

Cohen, Jeffrey. 1997. *Presidential Responsiveness and Public Policy-Making.* Ann Arbor: University of Michigan Press.

Corwin, Edward S. 1984. *The President: Office and Powers, 1787–1984: History and Analysis of Practice and Opinion.* New York: New York University Press.

Crowley, Donald W. 1987. "Judicial Review of Administrative Agencies: Does the Type of Agency Matter." *Western Political Quarterly* 31:265–83.

Dahl, Robert A. 1957. "Decision-making in a Democracy: The Supreme Court as a National Policymaker." *Journal of Public Law* 6:279–95.

Deen, Rebecca A., Joseph Igagni, and James Meernik. 2000. "Presidential Influence on the Supreme Court: Solicitor General as Amicus." Presented at the annual meeting of the American Political Science Association, Washington, DC.

Devins, Neal. 1994. "Unitariness and Independence: Solicitor General Control Over Independent Agency Litigation." *California Law Review* 82: 255–327.

Ducat, Craig R., and Robert L. Dudley. 1989(a). "Federal District Judges and Presidential Power During the Postwar Era." *Journal of Politics* 51:98–118.

Ducat, Craig R., and Robert L. Dudley. 1989(b). "Federal Judges and Presidential Power: Truman to Reagan." *Akron Law Review* 22: 561–98.

Edwards, George C. 1980. *Presidential Influence in Congress.* San Francisco: WH Freeman Press.

Edwards, George C. 1983. *The Public Presidency: The Pursuit of Popular Support.* New York: St. Martin's Press.

Edwards, George C. 1985. "Presidential Policy Making." In *The Presidency and Public Policy Making*, eds. George C. Edwards, Steven A. Shull, and Norman C. Thomas. Pittsburgh: University of Pittsburgh Press.

Edwards, George C. and Stephen J. Wayne. 1985. *Presidential Leadership: Politics and Policy Making.* New York: St. Martin's Press.

Edwards, George C. 1989. *At the Margins: Presidential Leadership of Congress.* New Haven: Yale University Press.

Edwards, George C. and Stephen J. Wayne. 1994. *Presidential Leadership: Politics and Policy Making.* New York: St. Martin's Press.

Edwards, George C. 1996. "Presidential Rhetoric: What Difference Does it Make?" In *Beyond the Rhetorical Presidency,* ed. Martin J. Medhurst. College Station: Texas A&M University Press.

Epstein, Lee and Carol Mershon. 1995. "Measuring Political Preferences." *American Journal of Political Science* 40: 261–94.

Epstein, Lee, Jeffrey Segal, Harold Spaeth, and Thomas Walker. 1996. *The Supreme Court Compendium: Data, Decisions, and Developments.* Washington, D.C.: Congressional Quarterly Press.

Epstein, Lee and Jack Knight. 1998. *The Choices Justices Make.* Washington, D.C.: CQ Press.

Eskridge, Jr., William N. 1991. "Reneging on History? Playing the Court/Congress/President Civil Rights Game." *California Law Review* 79:613–84.

Flemming, Roy B., and B. Dan Wood. 1997. "The Public and the Supreme Court: Individual Justice Responsiveness to American Policy Moods." *American Journal of Political Science* 41:468–98.

Friedrich, Robert J. 1982. "In Defense of Multiplicative Terms In Multiple Regression Equations." *American Journal of Political Science* 26: 797–833.

Funston, Richard. 1975. "The Supreme Court and Critical Elections." *American Political Science Review* 69:795–811.

Gely, Raphael, and Pablo T. Spiller. 1990. "A Rational Choice Theory of Supreme Court Statutory Decisions: The *State Farm* and *Grove City* Cases." *Journal of Law Economics and Organization* 6:263–300.

Gely, Raphael, and Pablo T. Spiller. 1992. "The Political Economy of Supreme Court Constitutional Decisions: The Case of Roosevelt's Court-Packing Plan." *International Review of Law and Economics* 12:45–67.

Genovese, Michael A. 1980. *The Supreme Court, the Constitution, and Presidential Power.* Lanham, MD: University Press of America.

Goldman, Sheldon. 1989. "Judicial Appointments and the Presidential Agenda." In *The Presidency in American Politics,* eds. Paul Brace, Christine B. Harrington, and Gary King. New York: New York University Press.

Handberg, Roger. 1979. "The Supreme Court and Administrative Agencies: 1965–1978." *Journal of Contemporary Law* 6:161–76.

Hart, Roderick P. 1987. *The Sound of Leadership: Presidential Communication in the Modern Age.* Chicago: University of Chicago Press.

Heckman, James J. 1979. "Sample Selection Bias as a Specification Error." *Econometrica* 47(1):153–61.

James, Patrick and John R. ONeal. 1991. "The Influence of Domestic and International Politics on the President's Use of Force." *Journal of Conflict Resolution* 35(2):307–32.

Kearney, Richard C., and Reginald S. Sheehan. 1992. "Supreme Court Decision Making: The Impact of Court Composition on State and Local Government Litigation." *Journal of Politics* 54: 1009–25.

Kernell, Samuel. 1986. *Going Public: New Strategies of Presidential Leadership.* Washington, D.C.: CQ Press.

Kessel, John H. 1974. "The Parameters of Presidential Politics." *Social Science Quarterly* 55:8–24.

King, Gary. 1993. "The Methodology of Presidential Research." In *Researching the Presidency*, eds. George C. Edwards III, John H. Kessel, and Bert A. Rockman. Pittsburgh: University of Pittsburgh Press.

Light, Paul C. 1991. *The President's Agenda: Domestic Policy Choice From Kennedy to Reagan.* Baltimore: The Johns Hopkins University Press.

Link, Michael W. 1995. "Tracking Public Mood in the Supreme Court: Cross-Time Analysis of Criminal Procedure and Civil Rights Cases." *Political Research Quarterly* 48:61–78.

McGinnis, John, O. 1993. "Constitutional Review by the Executive in Foreign Affairs and War Powers: A Consequence of Rational Choice in the Separation of Powers." *Law and Contemporary Problems* 56(4):293–325.

McGuire, Kevin T. 1998. "Explaining Executive Success in the U.S. Supreme Court." *Political Research Quarterly* 51:505–26.

Medhurst, Martin J. 1993. *Dwight D. Eisenhower: Strategic Communicator.* Westport: Greenwood Press.

Meinhold, Stephen S. and Steven A. Shull. 1998. "Policy Congruence Between the President and the Solicitor General." *Political Research Quarterly* 51:527–37.

Mishler, William and Reginald S. Sheehan. 1993. "The Supreme Court as a Countermajoritarian Institution? The Impact of Public Opinion On Supreme Court Decisions." *American Political Science Review* 87:87–101.

Mishler, William and Reginald S. Sheehan. 1996. "Public Opinion, the Attitudinal Model, and Supreme Court Decision Making: A Micro-Analytic Perspective." *Journal of Politics* 58:169–200.

Moe, Terry M. 1991. "The Politicized Presidency." In *The Managerial Presidency*, ed. James P. Pfiffner. Pacific Grove: Brooks/Cole Publishing.

Moe, Terry M. and Scott A. Wilson. 1994. "Presidents and the Politics of Structure." *Law and Contemporary Problems* 57:1–44.

Moe, Terry M. 1998. "The Presidency and the Bureaucracy: The Presidential Advantage." In *The Presidency and the Political System*, ed. Michael Nelson. Washington, D.C.: CQ Press.

Mondale, Walter F. 1975. *The Accountability of Power: Toward a Responsible Presidency*. New York: D. McKay Co.

Nelson, Michael, ed. 1989. *Congressional Quarterly's Guide to the Presidency*. Washington, D.C.: CQ Press.

Nelson, Michael, ed. 1995. *The Presidency and the Political System*. Washington, D.C.: CQ Press.

Neustadt, Richard E. 1980. *Presidential Power*. Revised Ed. New York: Wiley.

Neustadt, Richard E. 1990. *Presidential Power and the Modern Presidents*. New York: The Free Press.

Norman-Major, Kristen. 1994. "The Solicitor General: Executive Policy Agendas and the Court." *Albany Law Review* 57:1081–1109.

Norpoth, Helmut and Jeffrey A. Segal. 1994. "Popular Influence on Supreme Court Decisions." *American Political Science Review* 87: 711–14.

Ostrom, Charles W., Jr. and Brian L. Job. 1986. "The President and the Political Use of Force." *American Political Science Review* 80(2):541–66.

Perry, H.W., Jr. 1991. *Deciding to Decide: Agenda Setting in the United States Supreme Court*. Cambridge: Harvard University Press.

Powell, Lewis F. 1995. "The Supreme Court and the Presidency." In *Problems and Policies of American Presidents*, ed. Kenneth W. Thompson. Lanham, MD: University Press of America.

Pritchett, Herman. 1948. *The Roosevelt Court: A Study in Judicial Politics and Values 1937–1947.* New York: MacMillan.

Provine, Doris Marie. 1980. *Case Selection in the United States Supreme Court.* Chicago: University of Chicago Press.

Puro, Steven. 1981. "The United States as Amicus Curiae." In *Courts, Law and the Judicial Process,* ed. Sidney Ulmer. New York: Free Press.

Ragsdale, Lyn. 1998. "Studying the Presidency: Why Presidents Need Political Scientists." In *The Presidency and the Political System,* ed. Michael Nelson. Washington, D.C.: CQ Press.

Rehnquist, William H. 1986. "Constitutional Law and Public Opinion." *Suffolk University Law Review* 20:751–69.

Rehnquist, William H. 1987. *The Supreme Court: How It Was, How It Is.* New York: William Morrow.

Rehnquist, William H. 2000. *Reflections on the History and Future of the Supreme Court of the United States,* Remarks of the Chief Justice— D.C. Circuit Judicial Conferences, Williamsburg, VA, June 16, 2000.

Rivers, Douglas and Nancy L. Rose. 1985. "Passing the President's Program: Public Opinion and Presidential Influence in Congress." *American Journal of Political Science* 29:183–96.

Rhode, David and Harold Spaeth. 1976. *Supreme Court Decision Making.* San Francisco: W. H. Freeman.

Romano, Roberta. 1994. "Comment on 'Presidents and the Politics of Structure.' " *Law and Contemporary Problems* 57:59–63.

Rossiter, Clinton. 1951. *The Supreme Court and the Commander in Chief.* Ithaca, NY: Cornell University Press.

Rourke, Francis. 1991. "Presidentializing the Bureaucracy: From Kennedy to Reagan." In *The Managerial Presidency,* ed. James P. Pfiffner. Pacific Grove: Brooks/Cole Publishing.

Salokar, Rebecca Mae. 1992. *The Solicitor General: The Politics of Law.* Philadelphia, PA: Temple University Press.

Schlesinger, Arthur M. 1973. *The Imperial Presidency.* Boston: Houghton Mifflin.

Schubert, Glendon. 1957. *The Presidency in the Courts.* Minneapolis, MN: University of Minnesota Press.

Scigliano, Robert. 1971. *The Supreme Court and the Presidency.* New York: Free Press.

Segal, Jeffrey A. and Cheryl Reedy. 1988. "The Supreme Court and Sex Discrimination: The Role of the Solicitor General." *Western Political Quarterly* 41:553–68.

Segal, Jeffrey A. 1988. "Amicus Curiae Briefs by the Solicitor General during the Warren and Burger Courts: A Research Note." *The Western Political Quarterly* 41:135–44.

Segal, Jeffrey, and Albert Cover. 1989. Ideological Values and the Votes of U.S. Supreme Court Justices. *American Political Science Review* 83(2):557–65.

Segal, Jeffrey A. 1990. "Supreme Court Support for the Solicitor General: The Effect of Presidential Appointments." *Western Political Quarterly* 43:137–52.

Segal, Jeffrey A. and Harold J. Spaeth. 1993. *The Supreme Court and the Attitudinal Model.* Cambridge: Cambridge University Press.

Segal, Jeffrey, Lee Epstein, Charles Cameron, and Harold Spaeth. 1995. "Ideological Values and the Votes of Justices Revisited." *Journal of Politics* 57(3):812–23.

Segal, Jeffrey A., Donald R. Songer, and Charles M. Cameron. 1995. "Decision Making on the U.S. Court of Appeals." In *Contemplating Courts,* ed. Lee Epstein. Washington, D.C.: CQ Press.

Segal, Jeffrey A. 1997. "Separation-of-Powers Games in the Positive Theory of Congress and Courts." *American Political Science Review* 91: 28–44.

Shapiro, Martin. 1968. *The Supreme Court and Administrative Agencies.* New York: The Free Press.

Sheehan, Reginald S. 1990. "Administrative Agencies and the Court: A Reexamination of the Impact of Agency Type on Decisional Outcomes." *Western Political Quarterly* 43: 875–85.

Sheehan, Reginald S. 1992. "Federal Agencies and the Supreme Court." *American Politics Quarterly* 20: 478–500.

Smith, Kent W. and M. S. Sasaki. 1979. "Decreasing Multicolinearity: A Method for Models with Multiplicative Functions." *Sociological Methods and Research,* 8:35–56.

Smith, Craig Allen and Kathy B. Smith. 1994. *The White House Speaks: Presidential Leadership as Persuasion.* Westport, CT: Praeger.

Spaeth, Harold. 1997. *United States Supreme Court Judicial Database, 1953–1995 Terms.* Ann Arbor, MI: ICPSR Study #9422.

Stidham, Ronald and Robert A. Carp. 1987. "Judges, Presidents, and Policy Choices: Exploring the Linkage." *Social Science Quarterly* 68:395–403.

Stimson, James A., Michael B. MacKuen, and Robert S. Erikson. 1995. "Dynamic Representation." *American Political Science Review* 89:543–65.

Sullivan, Terry. 1991. "The Bank Account Presidency: a New Measure and Evidence on the Temporal Path of Presidential Influence." *American Journal of Political Science* 35:686–723.

Tanenhaus, Joseph. 1960. "Supreme Court Attitudes Toward Federal Administrative Agencies." *Journal of Politics* 22:502–24.

Thomas, Norman C. and Joseph A. Pika. 1996. *The Politics of the Presidency.* Washington, D.C.: CQ Press.

Tribe, Lawrence H. 1985. *God Save this Honorable Court.* New York: Random House.

Wildavsky, Aaron. 1966. "The Two Presidencies." *Trans-Action* 4:7–14.

Witt, Elder. 1986. *A Different Justice: Reagan and the Supreme Court.* Washington, DC: CQ Press.

Witt, Elder. 1990. *Congressional Quarterly's Guide to the U.S. Supreme Court,* Second Edition. Washington, D.C.: Congressional Quarterly, Inc.

Yates, Jeff and Andrew Whitford. 1998. "Presidential Power and the United States Supreme Court." *Political Research Quarterly* 51:539–50.

Yates, Jeff. 1999. "Presidential Bureaucratic Power and Supreme Court Justice Voting." *Political Behavior* 21:349–66.

Zorn, Christopher J.W. 1997a. "U.S. Government Litigation Strategies in the Federal Appellate Courts." Ph.D. diss. Ohio State University.

Zorn, Christopher J.W. 1997b. "When (and Why) Does the U.S. Go to Court?" Presented at the annual meeting of the Midwest Political Science Association, Chicago, IL.

Zorn, Christopher J.W. 2002. "U.S. Government Litigation Strategies in the Federal Appellate Courts." *Political Research Quarterly* 54 (forthcoming).

Index